*M*uch has been written on the p
a Guide *structured in itinera*
and help the visitor to a more complet
*been wanting. This publication is an .... lacuna and even goes a
step further by providing interpretations of the sculpture, painting and architecture
of the two churches in their cultural and artistic context.*

*There have certainly been illustrious precedents, beginning with the sixteenth cen-
tury painter Dono Doni's* Descrizioni *(the text has unfortunately been lost) and that
of Fra Domenico di Pietralunga, whose work, as early as 1575, bore witness to the
fact that explanations were required in view of the artistic complexity and countless
stratifications to be found in this composite structure. In this new* Guide *arranged
in itineraries, the author has provided a brief summary of the fundamental phases
in the* Life of Saint Francis, *of the beginnings of the Franciscan movement and of
the Order, making it easier for the visitor to set the historical and religious events that
lay behind the rise and development of the complex in Assisi into their proper perspective.*

*Francis was a great mystic, but also a man of his times, in close contact with the great,
with poets and men of letters, as well as the poor and humble, and this is what has
been brought to the fore.*

*The same can be said of his followers, such as Brother Elias. In these pages an at-
tempt has been made to find traces of a probable participation on the part of Emperor Frederick II in the early construction phases of the two churches and the subsequent resolute efforts by the Friars, following the Emperor's excommunication, to
conceal or reject this participation.*

*In compiling these itineraries of art and history, an attempt has also been made to
throw light on what happened later to the complex and its works, particularly in the
fifteenth century when the Sacro Convento took on its present form, probably with
a view to reproposing the idea of the Celestial Jerusalem. This aspect has all too often
been ignored.*

One of the principal aims of this new Guide *is to acquaint the general public with
the controversies regarding not only the building phases but above all the famous pictorial cycles which now, seven centuries later, have not yet been put to rest. Art historians are still debating as to whether the frescoes are or are not by Giotto.*

The Guide *has therefore endeavored first of all to furnish an interpretation of the
various frescoes and decorations in terms of the religious story being told. In other
words it presents visitors with an itinerary that can help them understand the stories
and fortify their Faith in Christ, in His Church and in Saint Francis. Although
the more traditional interpretations have of course been given, others have been added.
The visit has been structured on itineraries based on what was probably the original
unified iconographic program drawn up before the paintings were begun.*

*Especially in the Upper Church an effort has been made to reconstruct various lev-
els of interpretation of the pictures (vertical, horizontal, by bay), meant initially to
help the Friars, and then the visitors, to better understand the Divine Word in its
various manifestations. From Creation, to the birth and death of Christ, to the foundation of His Church, up to the sanctification of Francis, in an organic vision of
the World and its story in the light of the Word of God. This unified vision has been
depicted by some of the greatest artists of the Middle Ages who thus created, in Assisi,
one of the principal centers of all western art.*

Father Gerhard Ruf

Ferruccio Canali

THE BASILICA
OF SAN FRANCESCO
IN ASSISI

224 color photos

7 plans and drawings of hypothetical reconstructions of

the various building phases of the pilgrimage church

from the 13th to the 15th century

BONECHI
edizioni il Turismo
FIRENZE - 1954

THE LIFE OF SAINT FRANCIS

Francis was born in 1182 (or 1181), son of Pietro di Bernardone, a wealthy textile merchant, and Pica, often described as being of noble birth. Pietro di Bernardone had particularly active trade relations with the fairs in France, which is probably why he wanted Francis to learn French and become acquainted with the stories of the *Round Table* and the *Chanson de Roland*. The young Francis was also taught Latin, but he does not seem to have been a particularly gifted writer (later he generally dictated and used the sign of the tau as his signature).

As a youth, Francis developed a passion for knights and for heroic deeds. He fought in the war against Perugia and after being captured by the enemy at Ponte San Giovanni was kept prisoner for all of 1202.

When he returned to Assisi, he decided to go to Puglia and once more try his fortunes as a man of arms. The captain he was to accompany however did not have enough money for the necessary clothing. In the various *Lives* mention is made of the episode in which *Francis Gives his Cloak to a Poor Man*, who may possibly have been the man who was to take him to Puglia, and not any man whatsoever.

Francis at the time was aiming at military success and depictions of his *Dream of His Father's House Gleaming with Shields*, as the *Legends* narrate, may allude to these ideals (although the dream has also been interpreted as the moment of Francis' conversion). His cocksureness irritated his friends: "I know I will become a great prince" he loved to say, or "Just wait, one day I will be worshiped by the entire world". He was right, but not for the same reasons.

By the time Francis reached Spoleto on his way to Puglia, he was running a high fever and had to return to Assisi. All his hopes of glory were brought to naught but thereafter the Saint thought of this episode as being on a par with the call of Paul by God. This is also one of the reasons why Francis was always particularly devoted to the Apostle of the People.

The fever, the delusion and this event profoundly changed his character and Francis withdrew into himself. After meditating at length he decided to go on a pilgrimage to Rome. Along the way he met a leper whose terrible condition deeply upset him. Francis kissed the leper's hand and back in Assisi went to the leper colony to visit the sick.

This was just one of the series of events which Bernardone, his father, could not understand or approve. His son distributed money and garments to the poor, kept company with lepers, wandered through the fields and took shelter in the ruined Chapel of San Damiano, staying there days on end. This is where Francis had his famous *Vision of the Crucifix* which convinced him to leave his father's house.

Called before the ecclesiastic court, Francis took off his clothes, thus renouncing all worldly goods, in the Piazza Maggiore of Assisi. This sanctioned, before the Authorities, the fact that the Saint was disinherited after his father had tried everything to convince him to abandon his "madness", even shutting him up in a small room in his house (now in the Chiesa Nuova).

Francis then moved to San

Lower Church, north transept, Cimabue, *Madonna and Child in Majesty*, detail, *Saint Francis*

Preceding page:
Upper Church, nave,
Jacopo Torriti, *Creation*

Upper Church, nave,
Giotto, *Saint Francis Renouncing
Worldly Goods*

Damiano and finished restoring it in 1208, after which he turned to the small ruined church of Santa Maria degli Angeli alla Porziuncola. In the meanwhile he had begun to preach, reciting and explaining the Gospels to the simple people, and exhorting them to live in poverty. His preaching attracted crowds and a rich man of Assisi, Bernardo da Quintavalle, (his house still exists) joined him, distributing his wealth to the poor. This was the first Franciscan movement whose members, as noted in the *Legend of the Three Companions*, "were unlike all others in their life and garments and almost seemed wild men. Following the dictum of the Gospels to the letter, they owned only one tunic and, if necessary, were happy to give that away too."

Devotion to a life of extreme poverty and his custom of preaching (which the Church forbid to lay members, such as Francis, who never took his vows) were two aspects which made the relations between the Franciscans and the ecclesiastic institutions extremely difficult. This also explains why in depicting the episodes of the *Life of Francis*, Francis is shown preaching to the birds and not to men so as not to disturb the established rules.

Even so Francis continued to preach and attract proselytes. This is why he wanted to write a *Rule* for his group, to be submitted for approval to the Pope (1210). This *First Rule* has not come down to us, but we know that it consisted of various excerpts from the Gospels and it contained nothing the College of Cardinals could take exception to.

Francis left for Rome with eleven followers (the correspondence of the number of eleven apostles, without Judas, and Christ/Francis is striking) to be received by Pope Innocent III. Enormous difficulties immediately arose. Investigations were begun and he was advised to enter an Order that already existed, to mitigate the poverty. But Francis reassured everyone: there was no risk of heresy for the Franciscans intended remaining within the Church subject to the will of the Pope.

The situation was highly explosive throughout Europe and Francis knew that his movement could survive only within the Church, despite the fact that there were points of contact in some of his visions with various movements considered heretical (the Waldenses, the Humiliati, the apocalyptic visions of Joachim of Fiore). The Papacy was highly suspicious of all these ferments and the resulting heresies and also suspected of Francis, the last in a series of figures whose disciplines of life and interpretations were of a doubtful orthodoxy. Innocent II long remained uncertain and did not grant real approval to the Franciscan rule, despite the fact that the *Approving of the Rule* is shown in the frescoes of Assisi. The Pope wanted Francis to preside over the new Franciscan movement which would remain subject to the ecclesiastics and to a cardinal in charge (at the time Ugolino de' Segni, the future Pope Gregory IX).

When they returned from Rome, Francis' group stopped at Rivotorto, near the leper colony Francis often visited. The place then became a new Franciscan meeting place. Francis began to take an interest in the political and social affairs in Assisi and obtained permission to preach in the city cathedral of San Rufino. His sermons were so outspoken against war and the lust for power of the Church that that evening Francis' companions who had stayed in Rivotorto had the *Vision of the Chariot of Fire*, in which Francis was seen as a new prophet Eli-

Upper Church, nave,
Giotto, *Francis Appearing at Arles*

jah. Thanks to Francis' sermons, various laws were passed in the city which forced the lords to renounce their feudal property, and the population of the villages was put on an equal standing with that in the city, outsiders were protected and precise parameters were set for taxes, so that the political exiles could return.

Francis' message spread rapidly, for he preached in the language of the people in the streets, squares, and churches, and he spoke of concrete things. This was when people began calling Francis "the Saint".

In 1211 the Franciscans returned to the Porziuncola, given to them by the monks of Subasio, and which became the permanent headquarters of the movement. The Friars Minor had to earn their food with the work of their hands (importance of manual labor) and beg only when travelling in order to preach.

The desire for poverty therefore did not spring from a desire for a beggarly life, but from the total rejection of money and the resulting temptations.

In 1212 Clare took her vows. Since they were bestowed upon her by Francis, a simple lay person and not a priest, further disagreements arose with the ecclesiastical hierarchy in Assisi. Clare was born in Assisi in 1194 and was of noble birth. In 1212 Francis gave her the chapel of San Damiano so she could live

Upper Church, nave,
Giotto, *Death of the Knight of Celano*

there in poverty with a few companions (the Second Franciscan Order was thus created, that of the Poor Clares, followed in 1221 by the so-called Third Order, those who did not actually follow Francis in his way of life). Francis gave Clare a *Rule*, with precepts similar to those of the friars, except for the obligation of the missionary life. The Poor Clares also had to

work to help their fellows and Pope Innocent III conceded to them the privilege of practicing evangelical poverty.

In 1212 Francis left for his first journey to the Holy Land but a storm blocked him in Dalmatia and he had to return. In May of 1213 he was in Romagna and in Montefeltro where Ottone dei Cattani count of Chiusi in the Casentino, gave him the mountain retreat of La Verna. He then returned to Assisi where the first Chapter of all of Francis' followers was called, so they could meet with the Master.

In those same years he started out for Morocco where he wanted to preach, but when he arrived in Spain he became so ill that he had to return to Assisi. Centuries later the Spanish king, Philip III, reinforced the bond between Spain and the Franciscans by commissioning a church in Assisi, the Chiesa Nuova, which was built on the site of Francis' father's house.

Back in Umbria Francis set about reorganizing the Movement to allow a certain number of cultured men to join. One of these was Thomas of Celano, who wrote the *Legenda prima*. The relationship between Francis and culture has always been interpreted in a rather reductive fashion, for he preached simplicity and was wary of learned disquisition. Actually his culture was not in the least wanting, even though with regards to

Upper Church, nave,
Giotto, *Saint Francis before Pope Honorius III*

the Holy Scriptures it lay outside theological teachings of the religious schools.

Francis interpreted the Bible and the Gospels in his own way, which at times differed from the interpretations of the ecclesiastical authorities. For example, for Francis, the Old Testament was not only the historical preparation for the New Testament (the coming of the Messiah), but its prefiguration, the allusion in other words to events or situations which were to happen in the life of Christ. The *Sacrifice of Isaac* prefigured the *Sacrifice of Christ*; *Joseph Sold by his Brothers* that of the *Betrayal of Judah*. (These biblical episodes in turn prefigured the coming of Francis). This interpretation was transmitted to the Franciscans and this is why at the end of the 13th century the frescoes on the walls of the upper church showed episodes from the Old and New Testaments and from

the *Life of Francis*, in close interdependent relation with each other. But Francis' culture also included the epic chivalric poems of his times and a knowledge of Latin and French. It was simply that he did not trust the learned men and their learned quibbles. In this particular moment however he did turn to some of them, probably in preparation for the subsequent involvement of the Franciscans within the University.

Contrasts within the Order however increased. Shortly after 1215 Francis succumbed to discouragement, feeling that no one, not even his followers, understood him. It was then that his *Sermon to the Birds* took place in Bevagna. The interpretation must be seen in various allegorical keys: as a manifestation of his immense love for Nature; as an allegory of the deafness of men (and, above all, 'his' followers) to his words; as

Upper Church, nave,
Giotto, *Miracle of the Woman Brought Back to Life*

Museum of the Basilica of Santa Maria degli Angeli, Saint Francis Master, *Saint Francis*

an 'ironic' answer to the prohibitions the ecclesiastical authorities set against his preaching. After the *Sermon* of Bevagna, which is shown as a real prodigy with the birds paying great attention to the Saint, legendary tales began to grow up around the figure of Francis, enriched by miracles that happened in the Marche. In 1216 Iacopo da Vitrì, who went to Perugia for the election of Pope Honorius III, gives us an interesting picture of the life and works of the Friars Minor who were Francis'

followers. At the time the Friars were highly thought of by the pope and the cardinals, in particular by Ugolino (later Gregory IX), their protector. Francis too went to the Umbrian city to ask the new pope to grant indulgence to those who attended the church of Santa Maria degli Angeli in Assisi. The question was a delicate one and the cardinals tried to persuade the Pope not to grant his request since indulgence could only be granted in the apostolic sanctuaries. Honorius III attempted to find a compromise and conceded it but for only one day a year, August 2nd. The Convent in Assisi was thus able to begin welcoming crowds of pilgrims. The general Chapter of the Franciscan Friars of 1217 once more confirmed the unconditional submission of the Franciscan movement to the Church of Rome, inviting bishops and cardinals to the Chapter. At this time the Franciscan missions that were to go throughout the world were definitively organized, and thus Italy, Europe and the Mediterranean were all thought of as countries to be evangelized. Brother Elias, one of the first followers of Francis and the man who would be so important in the organization of the Order after his death, was put in charge of the mission in Syria. He was an educated and energetic registrar, at home in the political circles of his time. He was well received in Syria, while the Friars who left for Germany, Hungary and France were severely persecuted.

Francis then turned to preaching in Italy and personally went to Siena, Bologna, La Verna, Rieti, Subiaco, Gaeta and as far as the shrine of San Michele sul Monte Gargano in Puglia where he had wanted to go as a young knight.

In the summer of 1219 Pope Honorius III decided to organize another Crusade to Egypt. Francis went to Ancona and after a long journey finally arrived in St. Jean d'Acre, where Brother Elias was probably waiting for him. Francis then continued his journey and when he arrived in the crusader camp in Damietta he advised the Christians not to attack the Arabs because they would be defeated. His prophecy came true (he had denounced the iniquity of the Crusaders) and he had to take shelter in Cairo, where he was treated with great respect. During his stay he participated in debates and in-depth studies with the intellectuals of the Koranic school. The entire event has been summed up, by the anti-Islamic tradition, in the famous *Dispute* between Francis and the imam with the miracle of the Saint passing over fire (a scene then taken from the story narrated by Bonaventure of Bagnoregio and shown on the walls of the upper church).

After a second trip to Syria and Palestine, to the holy places of the life of Christ, Francis had to rush back to Assisi when the rumor that he had died led to a serious crisis in the Franciscan Order. The heated debate which

Museum of the Basilica of Santa Maria degli Angeli, Cimabue, *Saint Francis*

was later to tear the Franciscan order in two was coming to a head. There were those who hoped for a total fidelity to poverty and the non-institutionalization of the Order (the Spirituals) and those who wanted a monastic rule (the Conventuals). From Venice Francis went to Bologna, where the noted jurist Accursius received the Friars Minor in his famous villa, and then continued on to Umbria. The Pope, in his efforts to calm the contrasts, decided that Francis was no longer to be minister general of the Order and entrusted this office to Pietro Cattani, one of Francis' first disciples who also held a degree in law. He was also canon of the cathedral of Assisi. In 1220-1221 Francis decided to write a new *Rule* with the help of his most trusted followers. These Franciscan regulations were worked out between 1210 and 1221, together with Brother Cesare of Speyer who was deeply versed in the Bible. As many authorities have noted, given the changing circumstances, this is a series of heart-felt invitations, rather than a series of admonitions, made by the Saint as a follow-up to the spiritual advice he had already drawn up in his *Admonitions*. Early in 1221 Francis once more went to Rome to submit his new text to Cardinal Ugolino, who however sharply criticized the new dictate of 1221 because of its lack of unity

Upper Church, nave,
Giotto, *The Confirmation of the Rule*
Below: Upper Church, nave,
Giotto, *The Canonization of Saint Francis*

and precision and convinced Francis to draw up a new one. The cardinal also tried to bring Francis (and the Franciscans) closer to Saint Dominic (and the Dominicans). He had them meet several times and even received them together, hoping to involve them in common projects but both men declined the invitation.

Back in the Porziuncola, where the minister general Pietro Cat-

Upper Church, nave, Giotto. *The Death of Saint Francis*
Below: Upper Church, nave, Giotto, *Saint Francis Appearing to Pope Gregory IX*

transformed from the point of view of organization and became much more monastic. Up to then the Friars had been simple preachers and could possess neither churches nor convents. Cardinal Ugolino and Brother Elias saw to it that the Friars Minor could begin to own property and above all could celebrate Mass after having taken the vows of priesthood. The result was that some friars, like Francis himself who never took the vows, were considered lay brothers, while others were ecclesiastical to all effects. Just as important was the fact that this was when the construction of real Franciscan convents owned by the Order itself and no longer entrusted to others (as was the case with the Porziuncola) began.

tani had in the meanwhile died, Francis was witness to the election of Brother Elias, a choice in which Cardinal Ugolino certainly must have played a part. This Chapter of 1221 is traditionally the one in which the Third Franciscan Order was created, the one of the members of the Fraternity of Penitence, that is of the 'lay brothers'.

In this Chapter the Franciscan Order was also profoundly

This may have been too much for Francis and he withdrew shortly thereafter to pray and meditate in solitude, in an impervious site on Monte Amiata. Here he created a new version of the *Rule*, which he discussed at length with Cardinal Ugolino, and it was finally approved by the Pope in November of 1223. The text differed greatly from the one of 1221 and the invitations and advice found in the former, were replaced by imperatives and succinct orders. To many, especially among the Spirituals, it seemed overly submissive to the desires of Ugolino and their discontent grew. Brother Leo,

Upper Church, nave,
Giotto, *Verification of the Stigmata*
On the right: Lower Church, nave,
Saint Francis Master, *Stigmata
of Saint Francis*

one of Francis' closest followers, was particularly troubled and Francis wrote him a letter, the famous *Chartula* now in the Archives of the Sacro Convento in Assisi, which has been variously interpreted. Some see it as a *Laud* to Christ which Francis wrote at the request of Brother Leo who felt himself tempted by the Demon and was in need of comfort. Others, like Sabatier, have stressed the fact that in the *Chartula* Francis repeated the possibility of separation from the Franciscan Movement which by then had been transformed into an institutional religious Order, to follow his own way which would allow him to follow the Lord (Leo was deeply unhappy with the progressive "monastization" of the Franciscans, as was Francis). The words of Francis were quite clear: "in whatever way seems to

you best to please the Lord and follow his vestiges and his poverty, do so with the blessing of Our Lord God and in a spirit of obedience to me". The *chartula* was signed, as was Francis' habit, with the tau. In the biblical tale of Ezechiel this was the Greek letter used by the avenging angel of God to mark the doors of those who were to escape death. Those who bore the sign of the tau, and followed God, were saved, according to Francis, from eternal damnation.

In December of that year Francis thought of a new way to celebrate Christmas "live". He discussed it with one of his friends, a knight named John who lived near the hermitage of Greccio. They decided to re-enact the Nativity (the *Crib of Greccio*) as a message on the meaning of the birth of Christ. This first Nativity scene is depicted in the frescoes in the upper church (scene XIII).

After the Chapter of 1224, the last in which Francis took part,

Lower Church, south transept, Pietro Lorenzetti, *Stigmata of Saint Francis*
On the left: **Upper Church, nave, Giotto,** *Stigmata of Saint Francis*

he withdrew to La Verna, accompanied by a peasant. Overcome with thirst during the trip, Francis indicated a miraculous spring (scene XIV in the upper church). Then Francis, who had stopped to rest under an oak, was surrounded by a host of celebrating birds (the *Sermon to the Birds* shown in scene XV of the Upper Basilica refers more to this episode than to the Sermon in Bevagna). When he finally reached the hermitage of La Verna, Francis withdrew in prayer to devote the entire period of Lent to devotion to the archangel Michael. This was when he received the miraculous gift of the stigmata from a Seraph. The same wounds that Christ had received when He was crucified were given to Francis on his hands, feet, ribs and head (scene XIX in the upper church).

This passage from the life of Saint Francis is currently being debated and constitutes, basically, an argument of Faith. In the last years of his life, the identification of Francis with the figure of the suffering Christ was practically total and the stigmata were seen as the last physical sign of this identification. Lay historians have expressed many doubts as to the reality of these wounds (as in the current case of the stigmata of Padre Pio), considering them either signs of the disease Francis had caught from the lepers, or a 'pious' invention dating to shortly after his death, meant to counteract the accusations of heresy the Dominicans launched against the Franciscans because of their desire, which included the Order, to identify Francis with Christ. For the Church, however, those stigmata were a miracle (which the Dominicans also attributed to Saint Dominic) which certified his sanctity and therefore the

Francis together with Christ and the Apostles was seen as an inimitable model.

Upon leaving La Verna, Francis decided to return to Assisi. His journey was marked by a series of unprecedented miracles of various kinds. This was an even clearer sign that in his life and work Francis was following in the footsteps of Christ.

His health undermined, Francis hoped to regain his strength at the Porziuncola. The first part of the famous *Canticle of the Creatures* dates to this period.

The *Canticle*, one of the high points of early poetry in Italian, was composed by Francis – with the literary aid of the 'poet' of the Franciscans, Brother Pacifico – over a period that ranged from 1224 to his death in 1226. In September of 1225, Francis felt himself getting weaker. Cardinal Ugolino invited him to Rieti where the Pope had taken refuge with his court and where doctors who could heal him were to be found. They tried everything, but nothing seemed to help. Francis wanted to try music, which in the classic tradition served as therapy, but his followers were afraid of a scandal.

Subsequently Francis went to Siena to see a famous ophthalmologist. Great crowds followed him wherever he went. Francis was worshiped by the people as well as by those in power and they were already arguing over his relics for their

Basilica of Santa Chiara, Master of Santa Chiara, panel with the *Stories of the Saint*. *Facing page:* Convent of San Francesco, Tesoro, Master of the Tesoro, panel of *Saint Francis with Four of his Miracles*, detail

fact that the saint was without equal. In the 14th century the Spirituals were even prohibited from imitating his poverty, and

The Canticle of the Creatures

Most high, omnipotent, good Lord
To Thee praise, glory,
Honor, and every benediction.
To Thee alone Most High do they belong,
And no man is worthy to pronounce Thy name.

Praise be to Thee, my Lord, with all Thy creatures.
Especially for Master Brother Sun
who illuminates the day for us. and
Thee Most High he manifests.

Praise be to Thee my Lord, for Sister Moon and for the stars
In Heaven Thou hast formed them,
shining, precious, fair.

Praised be to Thee, my Lord, for Brother Wind
For air and clouds, clear sky and all the weathers
through which Thou sustainest all Thy creatures. And the airy skies, so cloudy
and serene;
For every weather, be praised, for it is life-giving.

Praise be to Thee my Lord for Sister Water,
She is useful and humble, precious and pure.

Praise be to Thee my Lord for Brother Fire,
through him our night Thou dost enlighten,
and he is fair and merry, boisterous and strong.

Praise be to Thee my Lord for our sister Mother Earth,
who nourishes and sustains us all, bringing
forth abundant fruits and many-colored flowers
and herbs.

Praise be to Thee my Lord, for those who pardon grant
for love of Thee and bear infirmity
and tribulation,
Blessed be those who live in peace
For by Thee Most High they shall be crowned.

Praise be to Thee my Lord for our Sister Bodily Death
from whom no living man can flee;
Woe to those who die in mortal sin.
Blessed be they who shall be found in Thy most holy Will;
to them the second death can do no harm.

O bless and praise my Lord all creatures,
and thank and serve Him in deep humility.

Lower Church, view of the nave

miraculous power - pieces of his garment, even his hair and nails. He was dying when he returned to Assisi and was lodged in the Bishop's palace where he remained till just before he died in October 1226. In the last weeks of his life, his most devoted followers took down all his words so that they might serve as moral support for the Order after his death. Francis thus had a series of *Letters* drawn up.

Taken to the Porziuncola, Thomas of Celano narrates that "he went to encounter death singing". First though he dictated his *Testament* in which he repeated his complete devotion to Poverty and the purest evangelical message. Four years later Cardinal Ugolino, who became pope as Gregory IX in 1227, declared that the *Testament* was not binding for the Friars Minor and supplied a *Declaratio*, or interpretation of his own which mitigated the more subversive and anti-institutional aspects.

Literary tradition has handed down various smaller works in Latin as written by Francis (the *Rules*, the *Testament*, the *Admonitiones* to the brothers and the *Laudes dei*) and this *Canticle to Brother Sun* or *Laud of the Creatures* written in the Umbrian vernacular in a rhythmical prose in the fashion of the Biblical *Psalms*. The tradition found in 13th century texts (the *Legenda antiqua perusina* and the *Speculum perfectionis*) says that the *Canticle* was composed by Francis in 1224 in the Porziuncola, after a night of extreme suffering for grave illness to his eyes, made worse by the mice which had overrun his cell and were scurrying over his sores. Francis thought he was tempted by the Devil and after invoking God, he had a vision of a marvelous harmonious Nature, a laud of Creation, which was the source of the *Canticle*. Literary criticism tends to accept this tradition, for it is highly probable that a poetical composition of such elevation would have been inspired by an act of great penance.

A variety of poetical sources can be identified. The one dedicated to praise of Nature could go back to a night vision had by Francis; the 14th century sources mention the fact that the lines known as "*del perdono*" ("*of the pardon*") ("*Laudato si', mi' Signore, per quelli ke perdonano...*" "*Praise be to Thee my Lord for those who pardon grant for love of Thee*") were written after a controversy between the bishop and the Podestà of Assisi; the first part, a real *Hallelujah*, is countered by a second part (composed of "*Guai a quelli...*" "*Woe to them...*") which recalls the contemporary medieval concepts of the *Dies irae*, the Apocalypse of the Day of Judgement; the praise of death, which characterizes the final part of the composition, was supposedly taken from the words pronounced by Francis as he lay dying, which would move the final version of the entire *Canticle* to after 1226. The *Canticle* was thus composed by Francis with the literary aid of the 'poet' of the Franciscans, Brother Pacifico, at various times beginning in 1224. The part played by Brother Pacifico cannot be ignored. Before his conversion, the 'friar of the Franciscans" had been a poet and was crowned in the Capitol (Campidoglio) by Frederick II (this suggests therefore a series of contacts with the culture of the Sicilian school of poetry and with the court of the Emperor that cannot be disregarded). The *Canticle* was then finished by Pacifico after Francis' death.

The first part where God is praised through Creation, reveals a thorough knowledge of the sacred texts and of contemporary poetry. In addition to being a real prayer which touches on the highest points of Franciscan spirituality, the *Canticle* also sums up the cultural attitude of those followers who adapted and perfected the composition. Francis identified himself with a religiosity that was characterized by praise of the Creator-God rather than God, a dispenser of punishment (even though hints in this sense are also present). What matters most though is the fact that the Franciscan theological position was, from its beginnings, more interested in an evaluation of Nature and natural phenomena, as the manifestation and first way of knowledge of God, rather than in dealing with sophisticated philosophical questions (typical of the Scholastic Philosophy and the Dominicans). For Francis, God as such is hard to know, but He continuously reveals Himself to Man in the natural phenomena and Creation. This position was typical not only of the Old Testament, later adopted by Saint Paul and the mystics, but also came close to contemporary Islamic concepts (to be noted is the fact that all praise for animals or man is missing) with which Francis had become acquainted in Cairo and which still circulated at the court of Frederick II, where learned Muslims were present.

The *Canticle* moreover was drawn up to be recited by the Franciscan friars in the course of their sermons. It is no accident that it was written in the Umbrian vernacular, which was however softened by the compositions of the poets of the 'Sicilian School' of Frederick II. The general tone of the *Canticle* was inspired by folk traditions much like what the 'Sicilians' were doing (although little of their work remains with the exception of a few love lyrics, the only ones 'saved' by the later 'Stil Nuovo' Tuscan poets to avoid any 'embarrassing' political situations). In the first part of the *Canticle*, it was probably Brother Pacific who used some of the terms most characteristic of secular love poetry ("*splendore*", "*radiante*", "*clarità*", '*pretioso*" twice, "*bello*", "*casta*", "*coloriti*"), of courtly language ("*dignu*" as dignity, "*signore*", "*gloria*", "*honore*", "*laude*", "*humile*", "*robustoso*", "*forte*", "*governare*"), and also of the art and poetry of Provence ("*alluminare*", "*enalluminare*" (give light to) is a technical word also used for miniature painting). The metrical pattern used in the *Canticle* is typical not only of Biblical verse, but also of the rhythmic prose compositions found among the Jewish communities in the Middle Ages (the *melishah*). This is particularly interesting in the light of the fact that there were Jewish intellectuals at the court of Frederick II.

This intense and joyous prayer becomes not so much the emblem of Franciscan "simplicity", as the 'symbol' of the Franciscan ethos intent on using instruments available to everyone in discussing the most difficult themes, such as the knowledge of God, but also an ethos which was aiming at using and summarizing the most recent and varied cultural contributions.

The highest levels of spirituality and poetry in the Italian School are achieved by Assisi and by Umbria in this poem.

Crypt, view of the tomb of Saint Francis

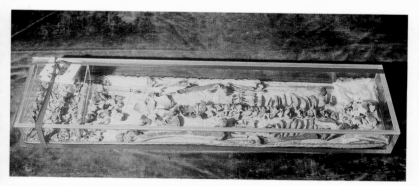

Crypt, the mortal remains of Saint Francis

THE COMPLEX OF THE PILGRIMAGE CHURCH OF SAN FRANCESCO

History of the construction of the Franciscan complex

Little is known of the initial phases of the pilgrimage church of San Francesco in Assisi, outside of the 'official' information the Franciscan Order passed on in the early centuries of its existence, highlighting some episodes and glossing over others, especially if they were more difficult to justify in view of the authority of the Roman Curia.

The place where the sanctuary church stands was still an isolated mound in the early 13th century, separated from the city by a drop in the land, where capital executions took place and where those condemned to death were publicly exposed. It was known as the *Colle dell'Inferno* or Hill of Hell. The Franciscans had probably already built a small oratory on this mound some years before, but after the death of Francis in 1226 the Conventuals and the Spirituals began to argue over what to do with this small cell. The body of the founder was in the Porziuncola where the Spirituals wanted it to stay, for the poverty of that settlement, so dear to Francis in life, ideally suited to his message. The Conventuals wanted to create a real pilgrimage church for the remains of their leader on the Colle dell'Inferno, outside the city walls and in a location that looked across the valley all the way to Perugia. It was just this site which would symbolically lay emphasis on the identification of Francis

Aerial view of the complex
Preceding page: **Entrance to the Lower Church, triangular wedge of the double portal,**
Saint Francis
On pages 22-23: **View of the complex from the valley below**

with Christ, who had died on the cross together with thieves, stressing the importance of preaching for the purification of sin and
death. The year 1228 was crucial and the victory of the Conventuals was confirmed with the intervention of Pope Gregory IX, even
though later years were to witness further bitter disagreements with
the Spirituals. The construction of a large pilgrimage church also
became necessary when Francis was proclaimed saint in 1228, with
all that this meant in the way of visits and pilgrimages to his sacred
remains. In March the Pope donated part of the land on the Hill to

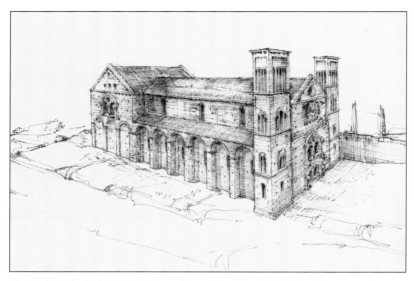

Plate 1: hypothetical reconstruction of the original plan for the Franciscan complex

Brother Elias for the building of the complex. In July the Pope himself laid the cornerstone, officially identifying the building as *ecclesia specialis*, a special church under the direct control of the Pope (a status it still retains).

What appears to the observer today as a highly articulated complex, capable of vying from a distance with the entire city of Assisi as it rises up in the landscape, is the fruit of enlargements over almost two centuries. What the original plans were is unknown. Some have suggested that it was probably the sharp slope of the land to suggest building the church on two superposed levels, the so-called lower church and the upper church, although this seems rather unlikely. By 1230 a first nucleus of the Basilica (which corresponds to the two aisles of the body of the present lower church) had been finished, and the body of Francis was translated and buried secretly for fear of theft (which is why all attempts at rediscovering it were vain until the early 19th century). In 1236 Brother Elias, at the time minister general of the Franciscan Order, donated a precious cross by Giunta Pisano to the basilica (later lost), while the emperor John of Brienne also sent gifts from the East (a beautiful altar frontal in embroidered silk is still in the Basilica Treasury). In 1253 the new

Plate 2: hypothetical aspect of the construction under the generalship of Brother Elias

pope, Innocent IV, officially consecrated the upper church, and authorized offerings to be made for the completion of the structure. On the basis of these few historical facts, the lower church has been dated to between 1228 and 1230, while the upper church may have been built under the Generalship of Brother Elias (1232-1239), or later, between 1250 and 1260.

Unlike most scholars, Giuseppe Rocchi (1982) does not believe that the upper church was part of the original plans. The entire question is centered on the nature of the covering and therefore on the thickness of the side walls of the nave of the lower church. If the vault initially planned for had been a barrel vault, rather than ribbed as it is now, this would have explained the thickness of the walls, with no need to justify them by the presence of an upper church. This theory still holds even in consideration of the fact that the side walls were from the beginning flanked by rectangular buttresses, later interrupted, on which the semicircular tower buttresses were subsequently built.

Rocchi also reproposed the question of the "entrance gallery", that is the atrium or narthex (41.5 m long and almost 11 m wide) of the lower church. It is generally believed that this space was

Plate 3: hypothetical reconstruction of the layout of the building after the entrance narthex was built

obtained by covering an old street that led to the Chiostro dei Morti, closing the centrally located original entrance to the lower church. (This was all before the area in front of the upper church was raised). Rocchi however believes that there never was an axial entrance to the lower church, despite tell-tale signs in the masonry. This is where he thinks the original apse of the early church was, on a higher level and with a crypt below (the present second entrance bay in the narthex, with a five-part vault, would correspond to this apse). Only later was the lower Basilica transformed into a church with two transepts: one for the entrance (narthex) in place of the initial apse and crypt, and one for the sanctuary. Recently Schenkluhn returned to the old idea of an "entrance gallery", with a hypothetical three bays for each of the two basilicas. The fourth or entrance bay would then have been added later.

Rocchi thinks that the entire complex was originally to have been one level only (the lower church) since the walls of the upper church are not perfectly aligned with those of the lower church, but project outwards and are reinforced by the two semicircular tower buttresses. Rocchi thus agrees with Thode and his affirmation of

Plate 4: hypothetical aspect of the extension of the Franciscan convent at the end of the fourteenth century

1914, that the two churches were built in two different periods and not on a single initial program. To resolve the load on the lower structure, the walls of the upper church were thin (in addition getting thinner the higher they go) with clustered columns along the sides of the nave, cylindrical tower buttresses and flying buttresses outside to transfer the load away from the walls, and with light ribbed vaulting. This approach to resolving the problems involved in load-bearing structures was typical of the great French Gothic architecture.

The entire lower church could certainly not have been built in the two years between 1228 and 1230. The frescoes there were not begun prior to 1255-1260. Would thirty years have passed before the painting was begun?

The general opinion is that no real solutions were found for the entrance part of the upper church for quite some time. It was finally resolved by attaching a half column which did not even touch ground on the inner walls in the area just before the first bay. The history of the facade therefore seems to have been rather complex, and after having been interrupted, it was later terminated perhaps thanks to Angevin patronage. The entrance to the lower church and

Plate 5: hypothetical reconstruction of the convent as it was in the early fifteenth century

the side chapels there, as well as the upper transept, were also under their patronage.

Although more is now known about the various building phases thanks to Rocchi's careful analyses of the structures of the Franciscan complex, just what happened in the construction processes, when they were carried out, what the original intentions were and who commissioned them remain problematical.

In 1985 the architectural historian Renato Bonelli reconsidered the entire problem of the construction of the Franciscan basilica, highlighting the complexity of the structural phases as well as the interruptions and changes in the construction yard. Bonelli believes that the lower church consisted of the first three bays, initially covered with barrel vaulting, and with powerful side walls which would demonstrate – contrary to Rocchi's thesis – that the upper church had been planned from the beginning. According to Bonelli there was a change in the overall plan between 1232 and 1239, under the generalship of Brother Elias, with a view to enlarging the entire complex and making it more monumental. At this time the transept was added as well as the structures for the four towers, the cylindrical tower buttresses, internal piers and cross vaulting. Under

Plate 6: the Franciscan convent after the middle of the fifteenth century

the generalship of Aymone of Faversham (1241-1244) the upper church was erected, to provide the complex with a more European dimension, adopting the skeletal structure (carrying piers and light non load-bearing walls) of the northern Gothic architecture of France and England. Around 1250, according to Bonelli, there was a third change in the project, more in line with the Franciscan ideal of poverty, in which the plan was for a wooden roof over the upper church. Around 1260 still another change took place with a vaulted covering of the upper nave while around 1270 the narthex of the lower church was finally built and then the first corresponding bay in the upper church, with an Umbrian type facade, as well as the addition of the bell tower. The flying buttresses were then added at the end of the 13th century to counterbalance the thrust of the upper vaulting, and the side chapels of the lower church were installed.

The interpretations of only two contemporary historians have been presented, but an analysis of their results clearly shows that neither available documents, nor an accurate interpretation of the various building phases to be identified on the walls of the building really tell us what happened.

Various other aspects can however still be taken into consideration. No trace remains of the small chapel the Franciscans had on the Colle dell'Inferno, where they gave spiritual assistance to those condemned to death. It was probably enlarged between 1228 and 1230 when the mortal remains of the saint were temporarily moved here. What was to be done with the site must not have been altogether clear yet and this was when offerings began to be collected for a building in keeping with the expected throngs of pilgrims. Brother Elias was one of the most important intermediaries of the peace made between Frederick II and Pope Gregory IX in 1234. There must have been a change in the workshop of the Franciscan *Ecclesia specialis*, probably thanks to the patronage of the Emperor (who also had to 'atone for' the fact that he had not participated in the Crusade of 1227). The bequest left by John of Brienne, Frederick's father-in-law, who wanted to be buried in the lower church in Assisi, was added to the emperor's patronage and the complex could thus also be thought of as an 'imperial church'.

Those were the years in which work was also going on, thanks to the contributions of Frederick, in the important construction yard of the cathedral of Trani in Puglia. The cathedral had been begun in 1097 in honor of Saint Peregrinus (Nicola Pellegrino, canonized in 1096) and was not to be finished until the middle of the 13th century. A series of rather unique features characterize this cathedral, including the highly significant fact that it was built as two superposed churches. Analogies both as to type and function and chronology with the church in Assisi are particularly stimulating for further hypotheses on the Franciscan structure. Entrance to the lower church in Trani is through an ample portal on the main facade. Above it is a spacious terrace which, like most of the upper church, was built in the 13th century. It should be noted that in Assisi the earth which now forms the area in front of the upper church was mostly brought there in later centuries (Plates 1-6) and that, in the outermost part of the narthex of the lower church, signs of the embrasures of the original central portal are still visible (denied by Rocchi, but see the *plan* of the lower church presented by him). In Trani, the portal leads into a transversal narthex, open on either side to the exterior and with two rectangular spaces corresponding to the foundation structures of two towers in the facade near the entrance. This was a typical feature of Norman-Swabian architecture (examples are the cathedrals of Cefalù, of Monreale and of Palermo, a widespread feature in Northern Europe and then imported into southern Italy). In the 13th century these towers were then turned into substructures for

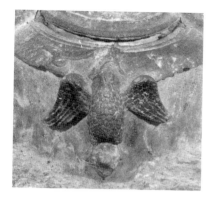

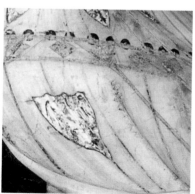

*Eagles as imperial emblems
(less probably of Pope Gregory IX)
in the Franciscan complex:*
Above: **base of the pilaster
on the inner facade of the Upper Church;**
Center: **detail of the stringcourse
on the facade of the Upper Church.**
Below: **Lower Church,
Chapel of San Martino,
Simone Martini,**
Saint Martin Renouncing Arms,
detail of the emperor's tent

the entrance staircase to the upper church.

In Assisi too, despite the greater width of the narthex when compared to that of Trani, it is clear that towers were originally planned for either side of the portal (one can still be seen outside, for in the 17th century an aedicule was built on top. See the *plan* of the lower church).

This idea for the basilica of Assisi might have been unique if the example of Trani had remained isolated in Frederick II's southern Empire. However the church of San Francesco in Gallipoli, also 13th century in plan although it was greatly modified in the 17th century, has two side towers on the facade with a large semicircular opening on the lower part as if it were an entrance to a lower church (in this case however the body of an upper church was never built).

The two side towers in the facade must also have been part of the original project for the Franciscan complex in Assisi. They were clearly modeled on architectural types to be found throughout the territories of the empire. It is no accident that one of the principles established by the Franciscan council of Narbonne, and restated in 1260 by Bonaventure of Bagnoregio, was that there were to be no free-standing towers (par.16) in the buildings of the order (with the exception of bell towers).

Hypothetical reconstruction of the Franciscan complex at the end of the fifteenth century and as planned for by Pope Sixtus IV

With regard to the hypothetical use of towers in Assisi, similarities with rare types of Byzantine churches to be found in Syria can also be established. After all, Brother Elias, General of the Order in Assisi during the construction of the basilica, had spent long years in Syria, still another way of emphasizing the bond between the Franciscan milieu and the Byzantine 'world' (of particular note moreover is the fact that the basilica of Sant'Apollinare in Classe in Ravenna at the time also had two tall symmetrical bell towers, although they were round, on either side of the atrium on the facade).

That those towers on the main facade were part of the original plan for San Francesco in Assisi becomes evident upon observation of a plan of the building at the level of the base of the piers of the upper church. In the inner facade, the piers bear crests with eagles, which have generally been thought to refer to the patronage of Pope Gregory IX (the imbricated eagle was the symbol of his family). Then as now, however, this is a highly ambiguous symbol, for the eagle is the imperial sign par excellence (in its twofold meaning it could here possibly be connected to the agreement between the Pope and the Emperor, before 1240). It therefore seems to be evident that the part of the upper church near the present entrance is not all that much

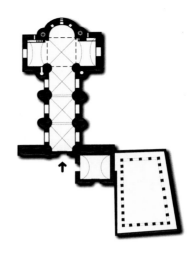

Hypothetical development of the Lower Church in the course of the thirteenth century.
A: the first layout with three bays and with the original Franciscan chapel near the cemetery

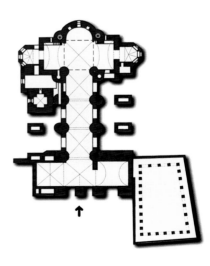

B: the construction of the narthex with entrance on the axis and the buttresses

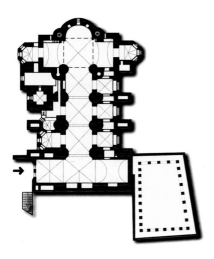

C: the narthex with the side entrance and the construction of the chapels

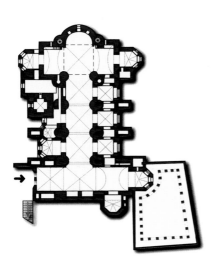

D: the construction of the last chapels

later than the rest of the nave and corresponds to the space between the towers incorporated into the church. Rocchi however believes that the facing of the innermost wall of the lower church was built first and that only afterwards was the outer facing of the facade of the upper church built, since the foundations of the two masonry curtain walls seem to be on different levels. But the fact that the genesis of the upper church was different from that of the lower church must also be considered, and this makes it impossible to say whether this diversity was really connected with a 'before' or an 'after'.

There is no doubt however that the towers on the facade were never finished. Work was interrupted at a certain point and their incompleted volumes in the upper church were never joined by that autonomous gallery which generally connected two towers. In Romanesque buildings this space was reserved for the rulers or notables who participated in the services and in Assisi may also have been planned as a papal loggia, as is the case with all the *Ecclesiae specialis* beginning with Saint Peter's. The same problem was to arise as late as the 20th century for the facade of Santa Maria degli Angeli. That loggia/gallery may not have been built because after 1239, when Frederick II was excommunicated and Brother Elias removed, it

Lower Church, narthex or atrium, fifteenth century cantoria

appeared too decidedly 'imperial'. The fact that sources, including Vasari, say that Frederick II sent the architect Jacopo Todesco or "ex Alemania" to work on the Franciscan complex must be taken at face value and would explain the typically Norman-Swabian styles and forms (brought in directly from the North or, more probably, through the mediation of the south Italian milieu). The rose window, of a typically Italian style close to the Cosmati examples in Rome, probably dates to about the middle of the century.

It is therefore highly likely that no autonomous entrance had initially been planned for the upper nave (or if it had been, it was certainly not monumental as the one there now). The upper church was originally supposed to be simply a large chapter hall for the Franciscan Order (something like the Sistine chapel in Rome, built at the end of the 15th century as a Council Hall) and was not planned as a place of pilgrimage. The entrance was solely for the friars who came in from the monastery behind the Basilica (the present transept), as the arrangement of the pictorial cycles inside clearly shows. Entering the lower church from the narthex, the scenes of the *Life of Christ* are to be found on the right wall, as was the custom for the Christological episodes (the right side was the side of Good) and thus, going into the upper church from the transept, as the monks did for the Chapter, on the right in the second register were the episodes of the *Life of Christ*, while the *Franciscan Stories* began, as should be, on the left part touching on the transept. When the iconographic program for the frescoes of the upper church were worked out and when they were begun (1265-70), the fact that entry was through the transept, and not from the present facade, must have been clear to all and then the scenes in the nave also followed suit to that initial layout.

The presbytery of the cathedral of Giovinazzo, in the Puglia of Frederick II, can furnish an idea of what the later exterior facade of the Chapter Hall looked like. Here the two towers on the facade are joined by a high decorated wall, without openings, with a loggia and straight termination above (in Assisi as in Trani, the entrance to the lower church, missing in Giovinazzo, was on that same

Lower Church, narthex or atrium, funeral monument to John of Brienne, in the intrados of the old entrance

side). It is not known whether, in this first project, the lower church in Assisi was to have had three aisles with cross vaulting, and massive retaining pylons, as in the Pugliese churches. In Trani the transept of the lower church was a martyrium for the earthly remains of Saint Nicola Pellegrino, and the pilgrims waited along the aisles, separated from the sanctuary. In Assisi, up to 1300 an iconostasis (a screen or partition) separated the transept of the monks (with the body of Francis beneath the altar) from that of the pilgrims.

Lower Church, nave, entrance to a side chapel

Nor is it certain what the transept of the lower church was like. Many scholars think it was added to the nave later, but just when is not known (even though it was certainly not much later). The way in which the two parts reacted to the 1997 earthquake also would seem to indicate a difference in building techniques.

Still another analogy between the cathedral of Trani and the Franciscan church of Assisi emerges from a comparison of the outer back walls. In both churches the semicircular apse is framed by two tall semicircular towers. In Assisi these towers were extended as initial buttresses along the entire external walls and seem to have been added later (but when?), as shown by the fact that the foundation level is much higher than that of the nave of the lower church. Initially they were to have been rectangular and not circular. If they had been built in this form (nothing but the foundation plinths remain), the analogy with the basilicas in Puglia, with imposing piers on the flanks, would have been even more obvious. The cylindrical towers in the apse, empty inside, had internal staircases and served to connect the lower and upper churches.

In the second half of the 13th century the circular towers along the side walls, as well as the bell tower, must already have been part of the whole. In the upper church the pictorial cycles were begun, including those in the nave, on the basis of a concept which identified that space as a chapter hall.

In the last years of the 13th century one more basic change in the plans of the two superimposed churches took place, surely a result of a more active patronage of the House of Anjou (they had replaced the Swabians in the South, inheriting commissions as well as teams of artisans). The first things to be built were the new great four-sided pylons (buttresses) set away from the walls and connected to the buildings by flying buttresses, crowned by watersheds and meant to counterbalance the thrusts of the vaults of the upper church. But above all this must have been the moment when, in agreement with the new Angevin rulers and the papal authorities, it was decided to change the whole concept of the building complex. The idea of allowing pilgrims into the upper church was advanced, as well as that of opening a series of private chapels in the lower church, abolishing the prohibitions the Franciscans had expressed in the middle of the century. A new large monumental entrance to the lower church was built to one side (Plate 3), replacing the axial entrance, which made the addition of new chapels as well as the re-adaptation of the space in the transept, where new vaulting was installed, possible. The end chapels of San Nicola and Saint John the Baptist were apparently added in different moments and new frescoes were painted. Whether the upper church had an apse comparable to that of the lower church is not known. The distinct differences in form, semicircular below and faceted above, indicate two different construction phases. The upper apse was probably added when the chapter hall was transformed into a basilica church. On the facade the space set aside for the towers, which had only been partially built, was exploited for the new entrance to the upper church, via a new monumental ramp, exactly as in Trani (where the bell tower was finished by the Angevin patrons), and thanks to the transformation of the original large two-light window of the chapter hall into a decorated portal, with a triangular gable at the top.

The back part of the chapter hall thus became the main facade of the autonomous upper church which was now canonically oriented to the east, towards Jerusalem. The pictorial decoration also seems to bear witness to the fact that the surface of the inner facade had

Twin entrance portal
to the Lower Church

never really been thought of as being part of the nave. The scenes of the *Franciscan Stories* (XIV and XV) found there are, from the point of view of realization and subject, autonomous from the others and were painted slightly later. That this surface must already have been there from the initial building phases however, is shown by the eagle emblems on the bases of the inner attached columns.

Work then was extended to the interior of the two churches where a great number of workshops were involved in the pictorial ornamentation until the plague of 1348 brought things to a halt.

By the last decades of the 14ᵗʰ century most of the structures of the convent were in their definitive form. In 1343 the donation of a plot of land south of the original complex led to the construction of a "new infirmary" by Gil de Albornoz. The "large western palace", originally a granary (from 1362) was also built for the cardinal, probably by the architect Matteo Gattapone.

The 15ᵗʰ century, too, was a moment of great transformation for the convent wing of the church. Practically all the new and imposing structures of the south zone were built in the course of the century, notably enlarging the extension of the complex.

Traditionally Brother Elias had already had a series of great arcades (substructures) built to support the hill in this area. At the beginning of the 15ᵗʰ century the appearance of the complex for those coming from the valley was less uniform and not nearly as imposing as it is today, and entry was through a gate near the bell tower. We know that in 1418 a new large refectory was to be built in the south wing, near the "New Infirmary" and using the same construction techniques. Just which building it was is not known. Probably it was the renovation of a series of structures (rooms) around the "Courtyard of the Immacolata" for work was expected to last no more than six months. In 1428 a refectory, known as "new refectory", was already in use but soon proved insufficient for the needs of the Brothers and the papal visitors.

A few decades later two other vast construction yards were opened for the building of the "large refectory" and the "South Palace" (later "friars dormitory"). The two structures presented a long passageway – known as il Calzo – above the substructures overlooking the valley (some of which may have reused those of Brother Elias). Many scholars date this to the 13th century (Brother Elias), at least in the first part, but most of it can be considered 15th century. There were aerial loggias similar to this in the old wings of the Convent (like the cross-vaulted passageway in the north part of

Entrance to the former Oratory of San Bernardino

the "large refectory", but they were later included in the new buildings.

The "South Palace" used as a refectory is particularly interesting architecturally for it has a large barrel vault over the upper nave. The vault and the building can be approximately dated to before the middle of the 15th century. But the works, even at that date, were certainly still not finished and the project was often interrupted. In 1471 most of the loggia had still not been finished and in

Detail of the frieze on the entrance porch of the Lower Church

1495 the portico remained unfinished on the south and on the west. At least thirteen arcades of the southeast dormitory had however been finished (Plates 5 and 6).

This wing was also particularly interesting. At the head stood the Oratory of San Bernardino, begun at least as early as 1459, which marked the furthermost point of expansion of the convent (the Oratory was then modified in the 17th century). It also seems to have had a spacious barrel vault of clear antiquarian taste.

No one knows who designed such an imposing and significant complex, creating a structure that was a landmark for those coming from the valley. The only names to appear in any 15th century documents regarding the construction yard are those of the masons, never of architects (even though Vasari mentions outstanding Florentine architects such as Michelozzo di Bartolomeo, Rossellino and Pontelli). The structural layout of the "large refectory" with the portico of the "Calzo" or its continuation (transferring the load from the main vault to the buttress pylons to which it was connected by smaller transversal barrel vaults) is not the only example of its kind in architectural planning of the 15th century. Leon Battista Alberti's Tempio Malatestiano in Rimini was to have had a covering of this sort. Alberti was closely bound to the Franciscan order and, according to Vasari, Bernardo Rossellino was his collaborator in the works commissioned by Pope Nicholas V in Rome. Moreover this type of aerial passageway is also described in Alberti's treatise, *De Re Aedificatoria* (VIII; VI,2).

Actually important works were being carried out on most of the Franciscan complex around those same years. Many of the roofs were redone between 1430 and 1440, most of them with cross vaulting, especially in the Palazzo dell'Albornoz, in which structural faults were apparently evident. An imposing barrel vault covered the large library hall here, but it was replaced in 1476 by cross-vaulted bays which would have been structurally sounder in case of earthquakes. In 1446 the staircases that led from the lower to the upper church were being worked on, making use of preexistent structures. Whether the fountain near the apse of the lower church, mentioned as late as 1408, was still there is not known. In the 1460s the "papal palace" to the northwest where the library now stands, was enlarged.

Work on the lower Piazza continued after the middle of the century (Plate 6). It had apparently been commissioned by Pope Nicholas V, making use of the substructures dating back to the Generalship of Brother Elias. By 1451 the City of Assisi, which owned the land and buildings, was able to rent various shops that had been built together with the portico. In 1472 another nineteen vaults of the portico were built next to the Oratory of San Bernardino, while in 1473 the wall towards the upper church square were reinforced, with the creation of ten vaults for shops (although in 1516 substructures were still missing below the Square). But above all those were the years in which the new entrance to the lower church was built, consisting of a new porch (years earlier mention had been made of simply a "vault"), now set against the enclosure wall of the monastery.

It is not known just when the entrance to the entire monastery, in the high wall that was initially frescoed, was moved to its present location. Originally the opening that led to the city of the "sacra" was near the bell tower. The fact that the upper part of the entrance porch to the lower church (in particular the decoration of the frieze) is incomplete, leads one to suspect that it was not isolated, but was the first bay of a new revetment which was meant to modernize and rationalize the southern flank of the lower church, marked by the projections and recesses of the chapels and the transept. The idea was however then abandoned.

A few years after work had been begun on the urban plan of the square, a new season of imposing works was undertaken by Pope Sixtus IV, through the Minister of the Franciscan Order Nani known as Sansone, and with considerable financial backing. New substructures were built towards the west, overlooking the valley, and work was done on the Chiostro Grande. It was in 1472, the year that Leon Battista Alberti died, that the new consolidation scarp wall along the cliff which was to jacket the "large west palace of Albornoz", was begun. The work was completed in four years, but other projects included the Chiostro Grande, the bordering spaces, the choirs of the basilicas, the "Chiostro dei Morti".

The continuation westwards of the large aerial passageway on the substructures, known as "del Calzo", and of the substructures themselves (which were modeled on descriptions of the walls of Jerusalem that appeared as early as the 14th century, in paintings such as Pietro Lorenzetti's *Way to Calvary*), stressed the Sistine desire to see the Franciscan complex as the new terrestrial Jerusalem and, in particular, the new Palace of King Solomon (with whom the Pope, who had a wing all his own in the Sacro Convento were he resided, tended to identify. The same was true for the King of Israel in the ancient Temple of Jerusalem).

Various parts of the Franciscan complex were destroyed in the earthquakes which never let the city be for very long. The complex as we see it now is therefore the sum of the subsequent restorations and transformations. In the 18th century the two flights of steps from the lower Piazza to the area in front of the upper church were completed (the staircase actually dates back to the second half of the 16th century but not in its present form). Some of the small houses which stood right on the lower Piazza were torn down and the massive restorations of 1926 in this area completely modified the backdrop for those coming from the city gates. Three large windows on the side wall of the former Oratory of San Bernardino (it had already been transformed into a dormitory in the 17th century) were opened and the enclosure wall of the complex was torn down.

Works carried out after the earthquake of 1997 on the other hand have tended to avoid redesigning the complex in any of its parts or to modify its appearance. Where possible, the precedent image has been restored while the static safety of the various structures has been ensured. A decision was made to 'relieve the weight' from the vaults of the upper church, consolidate the walls by injecting a special liquid mortar, and reconstruct the tottering pediment. The vault sections that had collapsed posed a real dilemma. The openings left by the quake have been closed and the vault sections have been rebuilt in their original forms, using thirty-five thousand bricks fired in the old kilns which still exist in Umbria. The composition of the material that fell was analyzed and new bricks were made from the same kind of clay. Traditional building techniques were employed but now it is all encased in a safety net of modern Kevlar fibers. The vaults have temporarily been painted in a neutral color, but the real problem is that of the pictorial decoration. For the time being, projectors have been installed which will project the pictures of the fallen frescoes on the vaults. It has been called the first "virtual restoration" and the first "Utopian workyard", but the purpose is that of restoring an artistic unity to the basilica without creating a simulated work of art.

Immediately after the earthquake the rubble on the floor was picked up, but the plaster, which fell from a height of over twenty meters, had crumbled when it struck ground. Much of it was lost when the material was collected. Even so over a hundred thousand pieces have been recovered, although they are small in size.

What was to be done? Leave the rebuilt vaults as they were, without decoration? Put on a new smooth or hatched intonaco, as is usually done for gaps in frescoes, to make them harmonize at least in color with the rest? Paint them with a starry sky as in other vaults in the Basilica, probably done throughout the centuries to replace what had fallen after other disastrous earthquakes? The problem has not yet been solved, but the Istituto Centrale del Restauro in Rome, charged with recovering the frescoes, had in any case decided to conserve, consolidate and list all the fragments collected, and try to put them back together like an enormous puzzle.

A computer is being employed in an attempt to identify the fragments with a view to recomposing them, guided by color, the nature of the brushstroke, materials, etc. rather than by their shape (in falling, the edges of the plaster fragments broke into such irregular, uneven shapes that they cannot possibly be precisely fitted together).

Basically this is an attempt at perfecting a scientific method, a computer program, which can be used for future traumas involving

Above: Upper Church, nave, detail of the consolidation in kevlar fibers applied to the extrados of the hanging vaults (1998-1999)
Below: detail of the tiebolts applied to the extrados of the vaults

works of art. Recomposing larger portions of the vault would seem to be an impossible task given the minute nature of the fragments. Hopefully some smaller parts can be put back together.

What we see today in the Franciscan basilica is therefore really the result of a sort of natural selection over the centuries, elements that have been 'saved' from the vicissitudes and catastrophes that have left their mark on the city. But it is also a mirror of the concepts of restoration and architecture over time, and how each work of art is also the product of the scientific methods and knowledge, as well as taste, involved in attempting to remedy whatever damage was inflicted. These interventions range from the modification or reconstruction or replacement of entire wings or parts with new 'modern' works, to the current attempts at comprehensive conservation, and the disconsolate and infinitely patient recomposition of the detached fragments.

The transept of the Upper Church after the earthquake of 1997

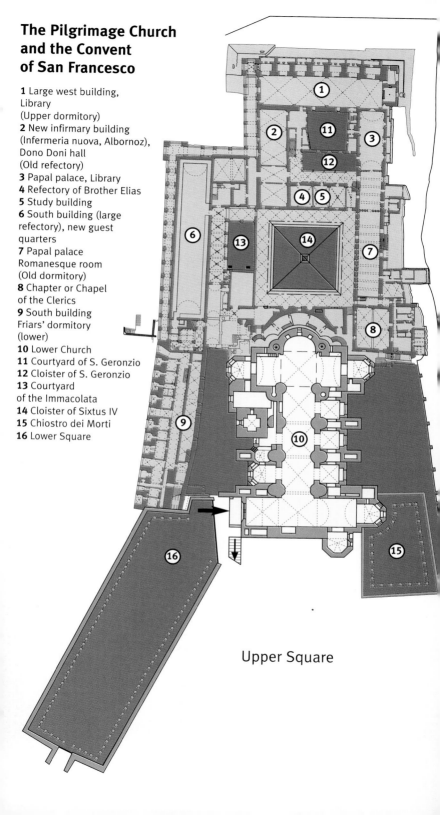

The Pilgrimage Church and the Convent of San Francesco

1 Large west building, Library (Upper dormitory)
2 New infirmary building (Infermeria nuova, Albornoz), Dono Doni hall (Old refectory)
3 Papal palace, Library
4 Refectory of Brother Elias
5 Study building
6 South building (large refectory), new guest quarters
7 Papal palace Romanesque room (Old dormitory)
8 Chapter or Chapel of the Clerics
9 South building Friars' dormitory (lower)
10 Lower Church
11 Courtyard of S. Geronzio
12 Cloister of S. Geronzio
13 Courtyard of the Immacolata
14 Cloister of Sixtus IV
15 Chiostro dei Morti
16 Lower Square

Upper Square

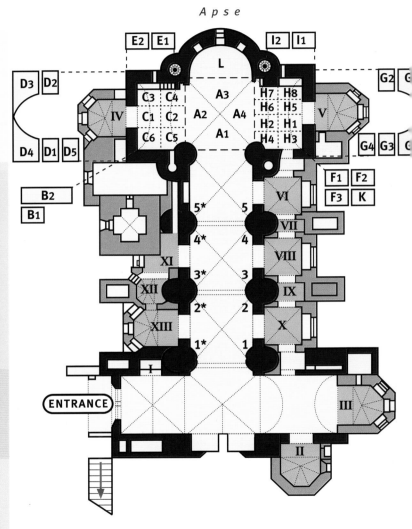

Apse

Transept

Nave

Atrium

Lower Square

E2 E1   I2 I1

L

D3 D2

G2 G

C3 C4   A3   H7 H8
C1 C2   A2 A4 H6 H5
C6 C5   A1   H2 H1
                H4 H3

IV   V

D4 D1 D5

G4 G3 G

B2

F1 F2
F3 K

B1

5* 5   VI

4* 4   VII

XI   VIII

XII   IX

X

2* 2   XIII

1* 1

I

ENTRANCE

III

II

Upper Square

LOWER CHURCH

NAVE

Frescoes on the North Wall

1   Preparation of the Cross with Christ
    Stripped of His Garments
2   Crucifixion
3   Deposition
4   Lamentation over the Body of Christ
5   Supper at Emmaus

Frescoes on the South Wall

1*   Francis Renouncing
     Worldly Goods
2*   Dream of Pope Innocent III
3*   Francis Preaching to the Birds
4*   Stigmata of Saint Francis
5*   Death of Saint Francis

CHAPELS

I   Chapel of San Sebastiano
II   Chapel of Sant'Antonio Abate
III   Chapel of Santa Caterina
IV   Chapel of San Giovanni Battista
V   Chapel of San Nicola
VI   Chapel of Santa Maria
      Maddalena

VII   Chapel of San Valentino
VIII Chapel of Sant'Antonio da Padova
IX   Chapel of San Lorenzo
X   Chapel of Santo Stefano
XI   Chapel of San Martino
XII   Fontana Chapel
XIII Chapel of San Pietro d'Alcantara

FRESCOES IN THE PRESBYTERY ZONE

A1   Vault with Allegory of Poverty
A2   Vault with Allegory of Chastity
     (Purity) of Francis
A3   Vault with the Glory of Francis
A4   Vault of the Allegory of the Obedience
     of Saint Francis
B1   Sunset Madonna
B2   Crucifixion
C1   Entry of Christ into Jerusalem
C2   Last Supper
C3   Washing of the Feet
C4   Capture of Christ in the Garden
C5   Flagellation
C6   Way to Calvary
D1   Deposition from the Cross
D2   Entombment
D3   Resurrection
D4   Descent of Christ to Hell
D5   Saints
E1   Stigmata of Saint Francis
E2   Hanging of Judah
F1   Maestà with the Christ Child
     Blessing and Saint Francis

F2   Crucifixion
F3   Blessed Franciscans in Adoration
G1   Annunciation
G2   Boy of Suessa Taken from the Ruins
     of his House
G3   Boy of Suessa Brought Back to Life
     by Saint Francis
G4   Saint Francis and Four Saints
H1   Visitation of Mary and Elisabeth
H2   Nativity
H3   Adoration of the Magi
H4   Presentation of Jesus in the Temple
H5   Massacre of the Innocents
H6   Flight to Egypt
H7   Christ among the Doctors
H8   Christ Returning to Nazareth
I1   A Child who was Unhurt after
     Falling from the Top of a House
I2   Francis and Death
K   Madonna and Child between
     Saint Stephen and Saint Ladislas
L   Last Judgement (apse)

THE LOWER CHURCH

The porch and the entrance

Entrance to the lower church is through a porch built by Francesco da Pietrasanta in the latter decades of the 15th century. The inscription in the frieze reads *"frater Franciscus Sanson generalis minorum fieri facit. 1487"*, but even if the celebratory text tells us that the work was commissioned by the General of the Friars Minor Francesco Nani known as Sansone, precisely when it was begun remains a mystery (for some scholars the project was by the architect Baccio Pontelli while others go back even further to the late 1460s). The porch was probably set against the great Gothic portal to protect it from the rain. But it is even more likely that it was part of a more general jacketing which was to have continued up to the transept of the basilica. The entrance portal has a central rose window with, below, two trilobate arches with a trumeau of small clustered columns between them. The stone decoration of the intrados or inner curve of the arches and the capitals is very rich, with *heads* that were probably portraits of notables of the time. It is generally believed that this monumental entrance was finished about 1270, but the style would seem to indicate Angevin patronage about thirty years later. In the spandrel below the rose window is a mosaic with the *Blessing Saint Francis*, by some attributed to Giovanni di Bonino, even the second decade of the fourteenth century (altough some say the Saint Francis Master). The wooden doors of the two great portals are decorated in relief with scenes from the *Life of Saint Francis* and *of Saint Clare*. The one on the right was carved in 1550, perhaps on a design by the most famous artist of the time, Dono Doni.

The entrance portal to the Lower Church
Preceding page: Chapel of Santo Stefano, stained glass window, detail
On pages 50-51: Lower Church, view of the nave

A) THE NARTHEX
(known also as ATRIUM or ENTRANCE BAY)

After passing the great portal one enters the large narthex (or atrium or entrance bay), over 40 m long, which precedes the actual basilica. A narthex was typical of early Christian and above all Byzantine churches and served as a place where the catechumens who had not yet been baptized or the penitents had to stay, taking part only visually in the ceremonies. By the end of the 13th century the narthex walls were decorated (a few plant motifs remain on the ribs), but only a few fragments are still extant. Between 1646 and

The juncture between the atrium (narthex) and the nave

1647 Cesare Sermei and Girolamo Martelli, the best painters in Assisi at the time, were called in to partially redecorate the walls of the narthex. The two *Angels holding back curtains* on the inner facade are a motif that was already quite common around the turn of the 13th century (see the relief of the neighboring *Monument to John of Brienne*). The 17th century painters then depicted the *Annunciation* and the *Adoration of the Shepherds* on the left wall, while on the right is the *Annunciation of the Birth of Francis by a Pilgrim*. Above the arch is *Saint Francis in Glory* while busts of popes who were protectors of the Franciscan Order are painted in the soffits. Up to the end of the 18th century the walls of the Fran-

View of the atrium-narthex

Narthex, Chapel of San Sebastiano

ciscan complex continued to be a privileged site where the finest artists of the city could contribute to the celebration of Franciscan glory.

The so-called *Chapel of San Sebastiano* opens off the left wall. This small space was created prior to 1542 and was then frescoed and decorated in 1646 with a canvas of the *Madonna and Child with Saint Sebastian* by Girolamo Martelli. The frescoes of the *Life of Saint Sebastian* (on the left: *Saint Sebastian Cared for by Irene*; on the right: *Saint Sebastian before Diocletian*) are also by Martelli.

Near the chapel, in the narthex, is a fresco of the *Madonna Enthroned with Saints* (*Anthony, Francis* on the left and *Rufinus* on the right) painted in 1422 by Ottaviano Nelli.

The fine monument on the right wall is known as the *Sepulcher of the Cerchi*. Its story seems rather controversial. The sarcophagus contains the remains of a notable of the Florentine Cerchi family (as revealed by the crests). The shrine itself is supported by five corbels and is composed of pieces of various provenience: the porphyry jar with handles is said to be a gift from a queen of Cyprus and Giorgio Vasari informs us that Nicola Pisano had a hand in its creation. Scholars from the 19th century on have tended to question Vasari's

Narthex, the Cerchi Monument

claims, for identification of that queen of Cyprus, whose name is given as "Ecuba" in a chronicle, has so far proved fruitless. In addition a 14th century date seems more likely than Vasari's 13th century one. It therefore seems more fitting to simply call it by its current name of the *Sepulcher of the Unknown Prince.* The Cerchi family undoubtedly reused pre-existent elements. Vasari's hypothesis that it was commissioned in the time of Emperor Frederick II, a period marked by artistic contacts between Cyprus and the West, must be taken at face value. The original monument, in Vasari's description, was composed of numerous figures with the queen seated on a lion to demonstrate her power. But despite the fact that the queen had left a great deal of money for the completion of the basilica, and that her monument was finished shortly before 1240, it was dismantled, probably after the excommunication of Frederick II, as being too 'secular' and connected to imperial power. Only a few parts, such as the jar with handles, were kept. They were then reused at the end of the century when burials in the lower church were once more acceptable. That this was not the original position of the tomb, which the Cerchi then took over, is also shown, on the back, by a filled-in monofore, as well as by various pieces, obviously from the monument of the queen of Cyprus, which have been reused in the adjacent shrine of *John of Brienne.*

Further on, along the right wall of the narthex, is a niche used as *cantoria.* In 1458 the Nepis family of Assisi probably commissioned the work from one of the Florentine artists in Assisi at the time (Michelozzo di Bartolomeo or Bernardo Rossellino). All that remains of this example of humanist art are the white and red marble bands and the majolica putti, even if badly deteriorated. At the time this *cantoria* was particularly important because the relic of the Holy Veil of the Madonna, carried in procession through the streets of the city, was exhibited here.

Narthex,
the fifteenth century cantoria

Narthex,
the Monument to John of Brienne

Next comes the *Monument to John of Brienne* (some say it is to Walter VI). In addition to being king of Jerusalem and Latin emperor of Constantinople, John was also a personal friend of Francis'. They had met below the walls of Damietta when Francis went to the Orient and John later went to Assisi when Francis was canonized in 1228. Since the attribution of this monument depends primarily on the armorial bearings with the cross of Jerusalem to be seen on the base, to some art historians it appears to be in Gothic style, even if it was probably made by a pupil of Giovanni Pisano, and they therefore suggest that it was a monument to *Philip of Courtenay*, who was also emperor of Constantinople. The question merits attention for if it was made for John of Brienne, the work may have been commissioned by Frederick II. John's daughter, Jolanda of Brienne, had married Frederick, bringing him as gift the title of "King of Jerusalem" and the monument may therefore have been commissioned by Jolanda or her husband after 1237 when John was buried in the lower church (would there also have been a tie between the interests of the Swabian monarchs in turning the Basilica into an imperial funerary church? This might explain why, in the 1260s, Bonaventure of Bagnoregio once more prohibited lay burials in the Basilica, forestalling attempts of this sort by the House of Anjou.) If this was commissioned by Frederick, then the possibility that Nicola Pisano designed it must be reconsidered, even though various pieces of sculpture come from different sources and the monument was not planned for its present location. Generally the complex is dated to the late 13th century, and is considered to be the work of a transalpine Gothic artist and another local artist (perhaps Rubeus). It is however obvious that the lower part of the base is earlier than the central group with the *Angels holding back curtains* and the reclining figure, here reused in a rather extemporaneous manner (note that the two *Angels* are not even the same height). The aedicule itself is disproportionate to the monumental complex as a whole, while the upper figures have been reused without any specific composition. The *Ruler*, his legs crossed in the fashion of the Angevin kings, has been set on a *lion* which, according to Vasari, was the one that supported the statue of the Queen of Cyprus.

Chapel of Sant'Antonio abate
The chapel of Saint Anthony Abbot, founded shortly before 1360, contains late 14th century Gothic tombs. The frescoes by Pace di Bartolo that originally decorated the walls have been lost. One can go outside into the adjacent Chiostro dei Morti from this chapel.

Chiostro dei Morti or Cemetery
In 1492-93, during the Generalship of Francesco Nani known as Sansone, it was decided to renovate the old cemetery of the Franciscan complex. (According to the inscription, it was Francesco Nani who had the entrance porch to the lower church finished and then had the great choir of the upper church built). The cloister wings with two orders were built, so that it was possible to go into the hollow space in the walls of the lower church from the upper passageway.

Chapel of Santa Caterina
Back in the narthex of the lower church, on the right is the *Chapel of Saint Catherine*, which forms the head of the narthex. The chapel was commissioned by the Franciscan Third Order in 1343. In 1362 the papal legate of Castilian origin, Gil de Albornoz (1305-1367), commissioned Matteo Gattapone, an architect from Gubbio, in close contact with the Spanish ecclesiastic circles, to turn this space into his burial chapel. The stone facing on the walls and possibly the ribbed vaulting are apparently by Gattapone. In 1368 (a year after the legate's death), the Albornoz heirs commissioned the Bolognese painter Andrea de' Bartoli to fresco the chapel with the

Narthex, view of the Chapel of Santa Caterina
Above: View of the Chiostro dei Morti

Narthex, Chapel of Santa Caterina, Andrea de' Bartoli, *Saint Catherine before the Emperor Maxentius*

Stories of Saint Catherine of Alexandria, who was particularly vener-
ated in the Middle Ages. The choice of an artist from Bologna was
undoubtedly due to the fact that in the period when the Papacy had
been transferred to Avignon in France ("Avignon captivity": 1309-
1378), the Spanish clergy met in Italy in the Collegio di Spagna in
Bologna, founded by Albornoz and designed by Gattapone (1365-

Narthex, Chapel of Santa Caterina, intrados of the entrance arch, Andrea de' Bartoli,
Saints and Cardinal Albornoz kneeling

1370). It may therefore be that the frescoes in the chapel were carried out in line with a precise iconographic-political program, particularly pertinent after the 'pacification' of the ecclesiastical territories by the Legate. The commission dates to 1368 but just when
they were painted is not known. In his systematic reacquisition of
the papal lands, Albornoz had concretely laid the foundations for

the reconstruction of an autonomous State of the Church, no longer under the control of the Anjou-Valois of France, and by 1367 Pope Urban V was able to return to Rome. That was however a brief parenthesis. The Italian notables, adversaries of the House of Anjou and backed by the Spanish monarchy and clergy (Castilian and Aragonese), considered Albornoz the main advocate of the independence of the Papacy. A few years later, the political nature of the pictorial cycle commissioned in 1368 by the heirs of the legate became clear. It was also at this time that Catherine Benincasa (1345-1380), a Dominican tertiary, later canonized as Saint Catherine of Siena, was publicly taking actions for peace within the Church. She and her followers, the 'Catherinians', requested a new Crusade (1373) and were loudly calling for the return of the Pope from Avignon (1376). After the definitive return of Pope Gregory XI to Rome (1378), the analogies between Caterina Benincasa and the older Saint Catherine of Alexandria came to the fore. Both were learned in philosophy and had therefore been subjected to relentless interrogations, as well as theological disputes. They were both mystics, thoroughly prepared in philosophy and doctrine. Catherine of Alexandria had converted the empress to the Christian faith, and had then been martyred, just as Catherine of Siena had convinced the popes to withdraw from French control (which had then led to the imprisonment of Pope Urban VI, and then the Schism of the West with the nomination of an Antipope by the House of Anjou). In 1375 Caterina Benincasa had received the stigmata, comparable to the wounds of martyrdom of the older Saint and to those of Saint Francis.

When Albornoz was removed from his tomb in the chapel in Assisi in 1372 (some say to Toledo, in Spain, and others to the Bologna Collegio), the space remained without an authoritative patron. Thanks to its pictorial decoration however the chapel continued to represent a precise and extremely valid phase in the political history of the Church. It is therefore not to be excluded that patronage passed to the Orsini who had commissioned the Chapel of San Nicola in the lower church a century earlier (at the time seconding the Angevin initiatives). The cult of Saint Catherine of Alexandria, which had never gone unheeded, gained momentum, probably because she was considered the patron saint of the faction which wanted the return of the Pope to Rome (in Florence the Alberti also dedicated a new Cappella all'Antella to the Saint). Devotion to the saint became even more fervid when new relics from Egypt arrived in Italy and Raimondello Orsini (1380) founded a center of the Catherine cult (1380) in Galatina, near Lecce. Orsini was a noble closely connected to the papal court of Urban VI, and had freed the pope from the Angevin attempt to keep him prisoner in Avignon. We know that a portrait of Raimondello Orsini had been frescoed in the lower church of Assisi because of his particular devotion to Saint Francis and his patronage. Apparently the portrait faded in the course of the years and it is no longer known just where it was. Figures of *Saints* and various scenes are frescoed on the intrados of the entrance arch to the chapel. On the right they include the *Conversion of the Empress Faustina in Prison*, and the *Martyrdom of Faustina*. On the left are the *Martyrdom of Saint Catherine* and the *Death and Glory of the Saint*. Specific episodes in the *Life of Catherine* are shown in the wall panels, with, on the right from the bottom up, the *Conversion of Catherine* and *Catherine before the Emperor Maxentius*. On the left is the *Philosophical Dispute of Saint Catherine in Defense of the Faith* and then the *Martyrdom of the Christian Philosophers*. The cycle is a celebration of the values of Faith and the integration of Philosophy and Faith, in line with a program that coincided with the foundation of the Collegio di Spagna in Bologna by Albornoz.

These frescoes by Andrea de' Bartoli are particularly vivacious, especially in the expressions of the figures. The portrait of Albornoz, shown at the feet of *Saint Sabinus¸* on the left side of the intrados of the entrance arch, is particularly interesting and naturalistic. Various personages alternate with the Albornoz coats of arms in the window splays.

Also to be noted in the chapel are the fine stained-glass windows with figures of *Saints*, attributed either to Bartoli, or to Giovanni di Bonino known as the Figline Master and therefore to be dated in the early decades of the 14th century.

B) THE LONGITUDINAL BODY
OF THE LOWER CHURCH: THE NAVE

The frescoes on the walls of the lower church are perfect examples of a didactic itinerary planned for pilgrims visiting the tomb of the Saint, in which the parallelism between the life of Francis and that of Christ is highlighted. This was a fundamental theme in Franciscan theology, and was the leitmotif, with variations, of the cycles in the lower and upper churches.

The great nave of the lower church is articulated into three spacious bays with cross vaulting, and for a long time, on account of the imposing structures, it was thought that the building was Romanesque, as compared to the typical Gothic style of the archi-

View of the nave

tecture of the upper church. Nowadays the lower church is generally thought to have been built as a large crypt to accommodate the
pilgrims coming to visit the mortal remains of Saint Francis, and
that its imposing structures were needed to carry the weight of the
upper church, planned at the same time.

In the middle of the 13th century this space consisted of one great
hall. Side chapels were added at the end of the century, and the
entrance openings obviously destroyed a good part of the wall frescoes, of which only fragments survive. Up to 1300 there had been
a partition or iconostasis before the sanctuary, to which pilgrims
had no access (it was located about at the back of the third bay). It
separated the area with the altar, that was used by the monks and
what was probably the first tomb of Saint Francis, from that of the
people. Early in the 14th century this iconostasis was torn down to
facilitate the flow of pilgrims. What it was like however can be
inferred from the scene of the *Crib in Greccio* in the upper church.
As early as the 13th century then the lower church was already being
radically transformed from its original form. According to Vasari,
the cross vaulting of the transept was torn down and the vaults were
rebuilt to give greater solidity to the entire building. It is likely that
initially there had been a transept which turned out to be too narrow when the side chapels were opened and which was then rebuilt

View of the nave

n its present form. The different building phases are evident in the way in which the barrel vaults in the transept act as counterpoint to the cross vaulting with its round arches in the nave. The side chapels were opened up at the end of the 13th century so that various notables could be buried inside the Franciscan complex – burial was prohibited for about thirty years between 1260 and 1290. The chapels were then joined to each other by intermediate passageways through the structures of the Basilica to facilitate the flow of pilgrims. In the following decades, the size of the buttresses then led to the creation of vestibules, used as minor chapels, in these passageways.

Between 1246 and 1266 the so-called Saint Francis Master, from Assisi, painted most of the frescoes on these walls, one of the main cycles of 13th century Italian painting (the Master of the Blue Crucifixes also worked with him). The painter was commissioned to do a series of panels with episodes from the *Life of Saint Francis* which would stress the parallelism between the life of the Saint and that of Christ, a story in pictures that would accompany the devotional itinerary of the pilgrims. This parallelism was definitively sanctioned by Pope Alexander IV. In 1237 Gregory IX had already admitted the reality of the stigmata, a highly controversial question which was of capital importance in this cycle to legitimate the identification Francis/Christ. The *Stories of Saint Francis* in the lower church were inspired by the story in the *Vita secunda* by Thomas o Celano of 1246, as shown by a *titulus* (or caption of one of the scenes) and the depiction of the *Discovery of the Stigmata on the Body of Francis*. The presence of the stigmata on the body of Francis, already maintained in the *Vita secunda*, was then taken up by Saint Bonaventure of Bagnoregio in his *Legenda maior* of 126 (which officially replaced the *Vita secunda* in 1266), on which the iconographic program for the episodes of the *Life of Saint Francis* in the upper church was then to be based. Since according to Thomas of Celano the stigmata were given to Francis by a seraph, while according to Bonaventure it was Christ himself, the presence in the scene in the lower church of the seraph alone has led to the dating of the entire work of the Saint Francis Master to a period between 1246 and 1266.

The reading of the episodes unrolls in line with a complex casuistry also used in the upper church.

Horizontally, in a continuous reading of the wall we have some o the salient episodes in the *Life of Christ* on the right, and scene from the *Life of Saint Francis* on the left.

A reading by bays establishes a relationship between the episode in the *Life of Christ* with those of the *Life of Saint Francis* on the opposite wall. Although this parallelism is incomplete because o the large openings that were created by the chapel entrances themes that are clearly interrelated can be identified and indicat that the choice of episodes was dictated by a specific iconograph ic program. Unfortunately their fragmentary state, with the mos important central part of every bay on the right wall missing, doe not allow a full evaluation of their relationship and quality. The work of the Saint Francis Master, with whom the Master of the Blue Crucifixes collaborated, constitutes one the of the firs known transpositions to central Italy of the new Byzantine realism and ductile flowing lines characteristic of the provincial Schools The monumentality of the scenes and the real space depicted brought the life of Christ into the 13th century and called to mind the surroundings in which Francis had lived no more than a few decades earlier. As in the products of the provincial Byzantine schools, the artist aims at the visual unity of the scene and space as such is dealt with (examples are the first attempts at depth of the ground floor or in the death bed of Christ). Of particula importance is the fact that the figures are no longer frontal, bu are shown in various positions and move with dynamic gestures This painter 'from Assisi' then fully anticipates what thirty year later were to be the 'innovations' of the workshop of the Francis can legend in the upper church, albeit with a different insight of realization and complexity of invention.

Fine ornamental patterns also appear on the ribs of the vault, while the glow of the starry skies is enhanced by the use of small mirrors in the plaster.

View of the nave from the choir

NORTH (or RIGHT) WALL OF THE NAVE: the *Stories of Chris.*

The opening of various chapels in the late 13th century unfortu
nately means that only a few fragments of the pictorial decoratior
of the *Life of Christ* have survived.

FIRST BAY
a) Horizontal reading of the cycle in the direction of the wall
In the first bay the scenes, on the right, show the *Preparation of th
Cross with Christ Stripped of His Garments* and, on the left, the *Cru
cifixion* (with *Christ Entrusting his Mother Mary to Saint John*).

b) Reading of the cycle by bay: the parallelism between the life c
Saint Francis and that of Christ.
The scenes on the two facing walls refer to the abandonment c
earthly things: *Francis Renouncing Worldly Goods* on the left wall an
Christ Stripped of His Garments Before Being Put on the Cross on th
right wall. The other two scenes are also interrelated since bot
depict the situation of the Church: in the *Crucifixion, Chri.*
entrusts *Mary,* who stands for the Church, to *Saint John* for sup
port; in the *Life of Saint Francis,* on the left, the *Dream of Innocer.*
III refers to *Francis* who sustains the Church.

From the left: **Nave, first bay, Saint Francis Master,** *Saint Francis Renouncing Worldly Goods* **and the** *Dream of Innocent III*

From the left: **nave, second bay, Saint Francis Master,** *Lamentation over the Body of Christ* **and the** *Deposition*

SECOND BAY

a) Horizontal reading of the cycle in the direction of the wall

On the right is the scene of the *Deposition* and on the left the *Lamentation over the Body of Christ.* In the *Lamentation* in particular, the Saint Francis Master achieves a high point in expressiveness in the careful rendering of textures. The body of Christ looks like polished ivory and sweeping folds of precious fabric envelop the figures of the pious women. To be noted also is the dynamically curving body of the grieving Mary.

b) Reading of the cycle by bay: the parallelism between the life of Saint Francis and that of Christ.

In the interrelated reading of the scene on the right wall and the one on the left wall, the *Deposition of Christ* (right) corresponds to the *Francis Preaching to the Birds* (left), stressing the crucial moment in which the first followers gathered around, and were in contemplation, respectively of the body of Christ and of the figure of Francis. This was the moment in which those who had Faith came to listen to a message that was valid for all of Creation. The scene of the *Lamentation over the Body of Christ*, to which the *Stigmata of Saint Francis*, on the left, corresponds, draws a parallel with the adoration of the body of Christ covered with wounds and that of Saint Francis, with wounds like those of Christ. In this case the parallelism between the two situations is powerfully underlined by the miraculous event of the stigmata of Francis.

THIRD BAY

a) Horizontal reading of the cycle in the direction of the wall

The *Apparition of Christ* or the *Supper at Emmaus* (the second scene has been lost) is still visible. The damaged fresco below with the *Madonna and Child* dates to the latter part of the 1250s, and originally decorated the tomb of Cardinal Pietro di Barro.

b) Reading of the cycle by bay: the parallelism between the life of Saint Francis and that of Christ.

In the third bay the *Recognition of the Resurrected Christ at the Supper in Emmaus by the Disciples* is countered, on the left wall, by the *Verification of the Stigmata on the Body of Francis*. Both Christ and Francis are subject to being recognized (for Christ the episode of Thomas who wants to touch the wounds to make sure they are real becomes particularly significant) something of which Faith has no need.

Nave, third bay, view of the right wall

SOUTH (or LEFT) WALL OF THE NAVE:
the *Stories of Saint Francis*

FIRST BAY
a) Horizontal reading of the cycle in the direction of the wall
The scenes in the first bay are, on the left, *Francis Renounces Worldly Goods*, and on the right, the *Dream of Pope Innocent III.*

SECOND BAY
a) Horizontal reading of the cycle in the direction of the wall
On the left is depicted the *Sermon to the Birds*, on the right, the *Stigmata of Saint Francis.*

From the left: **Nave, second bay, Saint Francis Master,** *Sermon to the Birds* **and the** *Stigmata of Saint Francis*

THIRD BAY
a) Horizontal reading of the cycle in the direction of the wall
Shown is the scene with the *Funeral of the Saint and the Verification of the Stigmata.*

The pulpit of Saint Stanislas is in the same bay.

The tribune or pulpit of Saint Stanislas
Up to 1300 the iconostasis, or partition which separated the space of the monks from that of the people, was attached to the wall where the niche in the form of a cantoria (tribune or pulpit) dedicated to Saint Stanislas is now located. The famous *Crucifix* paint-

Left: **Nave, tribune of Saint Stanislas or Cantoria, Puccio Capanna**
Right: **Nave, tribune of Saint Stanislas, Puccio Capanna,** *Crucifixion*

ed by Giunta Pisano for Brother Elias in 1236 (now lost) originally stood over the iconostasis. When it was dismantled, an opening
something like the entrance to the chapel of the Magdalene across
the way was set into the masonry (with the consequent destruction
of the 13th century frescoes) and decorated like a cantoria with the
marble slabs of the iconostasis. In 1337-1338 Puccio Capanna was
called in to paint the space of this altar where mass was said in
honor of Saint Stanislas, archbishop of Krakow, proclaimed saint in
Assisi in 1253. At the back is the *Coronation of the Virgin with
angelic choirs*, while in the soffit of the arch are two *Stories of Saint
Stanislas: Stanislas Bringing a Dead Man Back to Life so He can Bear
Witness to his Innocence before King Boleslas* and the *Martyrdom of
the Saint.* These paintings can be dated to the period immediately
following the artist's collaboration with the Giottesque masters in
the vault sections of the adjacent sanctuary. The unity of color,
space and expression in his figures mark a peak in the painter's oeuvre and this depiction of reality was then taken as model by much
of Gothic and late Gothic culture. Vasari mentions the painter as
one of Giotto's later pupils, one of the finest representatives of that
"sweet and unified" manner which was so popular before the middle of the 14th century. To be noted in particular is the architectural setting in the scene of the *Martyrdom of the Saint,* as his limbs are
being violently detached. The church in the scene has been identified as the upper church of Assisi (with, in the background, the
great *Cross* Giunta Pisano made for Brother Elias).

Left: **Nave, tribune of Saint Stanislas, Puccio Capanna,** *Saint Stanislas Bringing a Dead Person back to Life. On the right:* **Nave, tribune of Saint Stanislas, Puccio Capanna,** *Martyrdom of Saint Stanislas*

C) AREA OF THE SANCTUARY (PRESBYTERY)

Scholars have still not reached an agreement regarding the dates of the sanctuary area. For many it is contemporary with the building of the nave and should then fall into the period of the Generalship of Brother Elias, between 1228 and 1236. Others believe that the transept was added later, after a change in orientation of the church when the apse was moved from east to west. The architectural structures of the transept are clearly different from those of the nave. The presbytery is covered by a single large barrel vault, which turns into cross vaulting over the actual sanctuary, unlike the great cross vaults over each bay to be found in the nave. Vasari mentions that, at a certain point, some of the covering of the lower church was torn down and rebuilt because of static problems in the construction. It is probable that the arms of the transept were involved in a transformation of this kind so that only the central cross vault was left to transfer the weight to the four corners, while each of the new barrel vaults exploited the support of two whole walls, instead of four piers alone. The two symmetrical chapels (the one in the north arm dedicated to Saint Nicholas, and the one in the south wall dedicated to John the Baptist) were opened later, at the turn of the century. Vasari also states that they were done by Agnolo and Agostino from Siena. The apse too seems to have a rather varied history. It is probable that the Basilica originally had an apse with three conches, with the center one smaller than the one there now, like the cathedral of Trani in Puglia (the masonry and the overall exterior appearance would seem to indicate this). Probably when the round buttresses on the exterior walls of the nave were built, the two smaller side apses were used for this purpose (it is no accident that all the towers are hollow) and the central apse was consequently enlarged. Since these structures also had to support the apse structures of the upper church, an external ambulatory was created, like those in the basilicas across the Alps, to serve as buttressing.

The sanctuary area fits perfectly into a didactic itinerary meant for pilgrims and once more stresses the parallelism between the lives of Francis and Christ. The crux of the composition consists of the subjects decorating the cross vaults above the altar. *Scenes from the Life of Christ* are frescoed in the two arms of the transept, but their arrangement is unusual, for they are not in line with the normal chronological arrangement of His life. There should have been subjects referring to the *Passion* on the right of the nave, in the northern transept (because the right was the more important side) with those of the *Infancy* on the left, while it is exactly the reverse. The Franciscan themes on the vaulting of the central bay of the sanctuary also set the stage for the stories of Christ: the *Vault with the Allegory of the Obedience of Saint Francis*, on the left, is parallel to the maximum obedience of Christ to the design of God the Father up to his death and then Resurrection; the *Vault of the Allegory of Chastity (Purity) of Francis*, on the right, is connected with the *Stories of the Infancy of Christ* (infancy=purity). And then the *Vault with the Glory of Francis* was originally related with his *celestial Glory* and therefore with the mission entrusted to his followers by the saint. The *Vault with the Allegory of Poverty*, towards the nave, is connected with the episodes of the *Life of the Saint*, who had taken Poverty as the absolute criteria of his life.

No certain documents exist regarding the execution of the frescoes in the sanctuary area and all we have is what Vasari (over two hundred years later) has to say, and above all the analyses of art historians, beginning with Giovan Battista Cavalcaselle at the end of the 19th century. In other words no certain documents, no signatures, no evidence. The latest critical evaluations are concerned primarily with identification of the works by Cimabue (mentioned: 1272-1302), whose activity is testified to by important examples such as the *Maestà* (some historians believe that he even did much of the decoration of the entire transept, destroyed when the various chapels were opened and then completely redone), or the Saint Francis Master, who also worked on the nave walls.

View of the presbytery

Giotto's hand can be identified in the transept, although in a second phase with respect to his work in the upper church. There would be work by his students, the so-called "Giottesque Masters" (the frescoes in the right arm of the transept, in the chapel of San Nicola and in the cross vaulting of the presbytery would be by Giotto and his pupils) and Pietro Lorenzetti (1280/85-1348?) and his brother Ambrogio (1285-1348?) would have worked in the left arm of the transept.

Art historians tend to agree regarding these attributions as well as the succession of Giotto/Giottesque and Lorenzetti phases. Analysis of the plaster in the transept has led to the identification of a series of daily work patches (since only that part of the fresco which could be painted in a single day was plastered so that the surface would not dry out) which tell us in what direction the work was done. The frescoes were begun on the north (right) side of the transept, followed by the central crossing, and then, after an abrupt interruption of the Giottesque workshop (as shown by some of the busts of *Blessed* in the large arches of the central crossing), the left transept was done by the Lorenzetti. There are no doubts that after the walls of the upper church had been painted, the patrons also decided to redo the lower church in line with the latest fashions, especially once initiatives in the decoration of the lower church were no longer limited to the Order but open to private individuals. A taste for magnificence appears in the color contrasts and the use of gold, in the deep blues and the adoption, especially by the Sienese, of jewel-like effects which make this one of the most sumptuous of all 14th century spaces, almost like the inside of a great jeweler's shop. This taste for magnificence has only recently been re-evaluated by art historians, for up until then any kind of decorative enrichment and the "fairy-tale" atmosphere typical of Gothic art had been considered redundant and unnecessary, in the light of the styles of Giotto or Simone Martini (composed of plastic synthesis or elegant linear rhythms). Despite this re-evaluation, it is still difficult to say who the painters were. Problems regarding the Lorenzetti moreover are flanked by those regarding Cimabue and questions regarding Giotto and the Giottesque painters and, therefore, Simone Martini, and what was done here is closely related to what was happening in 14th century Tuscan painting.

VAULTS OF THE SANCTUARY (PRESBYTERY):
the guiding principles to the teachings of Saint Francis

The guiding principles to the life and teachings of Francis are shown at the end of the nave, right in the crossing over the altar, in a sort of synthesis that could easily be learned by heart and left as moral advice to his followers of all times.

Although the pictorial decoration of the crossing, darkened by the smoke of candles and altered in chiaroscuro and colors, has been cleaned frequently throughout the centuries, the smoke had gone too deep into the plaster to remove all traces. This makes the reading of many specific details in the frescoes difficult, above all regarding the 'hands' of the painters, to the point of naming a hypothetical "Blackish Painter". Most recently Bruno Zanardi has attributed the decoration of the vaults to Giottesque painters, masters active in the workshop of Giotto and his collaborators (including Ricco di Lapo, Angeletto da Gubbio, the "Expressionist Master of Santa Chiara" or Palmerino di Guido, and perhaps Stefano Fiorentino, despite the fact that he would have been very young at the time), whose art has been described as a "softened and expressive version of Giotto's art", around 1308-1310 and somewhat later. The vaults have also occasionally been connected with a commission on the part of Cardinal Stefaneschi, which would shift the date to 1334. Some art historians opt for a "Master of the Vaults" ("Maestro delle Vele"), who can be identified because his figures generally have their eyes wide open in ecstasy and marvel at the miraculous events. This painter can be identified with Giovanni di Bonino, who also did many stained glass windows. The work would have been carried out under Giotto's supervision, who may also have been working at the time in the northern transept and in the Chapel of the Magdalene nearby.

The ribs are decorated with the celestial hierarchies of *Angels*, while the *Messiah* is depicted in the central point on the vault.

The Allegory of Poverty. In the center of the vault section, *Christ* holds the right hand of *Poverty* as she reaches out to *Saint Francis* who, with divine benediction, is about to become her spouse. With her left hand, *Poverty* is offering a ring she has just received from *Hope*, while *Charity*, her head wreathed in roses, offers a heart to the newly wedded pair. In the lower register, there are various outstanding episodes relating to the concept of Poverty and in one way or other connected to the life of Francis. On the right, a *young man* offers his cloak to a beggar (clearly referring to the Story of Saint Martin and the *Homage of a Simple Man to Francis* – new Martin. On the left – the side of error – is a scene that counters that of *Charity*. Three revelers despise her as Francis had done in his youth. At the side an *angel* points out *Poverty* to a *figure* crowned with laurel and with a falcon, who is committing gestures of disdain. It might be an allusion to the emperor, Frederick II, after his excommunication (known also for his passion for falconry). The *Franciscan friar* accompanying him might be Brother Elias, who was particularly close to the emperor and was then also excommunicated. The presence of Frederick and Elias in this section might indicate that they had both wished to create a building that was too sumptuous for the remains of Francis and contrasted with his principle of poverty.

Presbytery, vault, Giottesque masters, *Allegory of Poverty*

Presbytery, vault, Giottesque masters, *Vault of Purity*

The Allegory of Purity or Chastity. In the vault towards the right transept, on the north, is the allegory of *Chastity*. She is shown enclosed in a castle, like the damsel of the chivalric poets, protected in the highest fortified tower, with two *Angels* bringing her a diadem and a palm, symbols of chastity. Outside the walls are armed warriors with shields, while *Purity* and *Strength of Soul* lean out of the castle offering gifts to a young man. On the right side of the scene, *Penitence Puts to Flight Devils and in Particular Carnal Love*, while on the left *Saint Francis Invites a Friar, a Poor Clare and a Lay Person to Enter the Sacred Space*. The three personages have been interpreted as the three branches of the Franciscan order (Tertiaries, Brothers Minor and Poor Clares), while the secular figure may be *Dante* who had dedicated the IX canto of *Paradise* of his *Divine Comedy* to Saint Francis and Poverty as spouses.

The Glory of Saint Francis. The intentions of the Franciscans to build a simple unadorned shrine were no longer acceptable in Assisi when the transept vaulting was painted. In this *Saint Francis in Glory* in particular the Giottesque Masters achieved an apex in their use of brilliant colors, above all in the return to a decidedly Byzantine taste for gold grounds, also typical of the latest fashions. The rows of *Angels* are an example of the poetical level of the Master of the Vaults (Maestro delle Vele) in his rendering of a dreamy and aesthetically elegant atmosphere, with gold-studded garments, refined colors and flesh tones that look like ivory. *Saint Francis* is shown

Presbytery, vault, Giottesque Masters, *Vault of the Glory of Saint Francis*

Presbytery, vault, Giottesque Masters, *Vault of Obedience*

beardless as in early Christian depictions of Christ, his eyes wide open in mystical ecstasy. He is seated on a throne wearing splendid garments, surrounded by hosts of *Angels*, almost as if he were a new Messiah, in a salvific vision of his role.

The Allegory of Obedience. The allegory of Obedience shows her in a loggia placing a yoke on a kneeling *Friar*. In the left bay of the log-

Presbytery, view of the altar

gia in which the scene takes place is the image of double-faced *Prudence*, with a compass, mirror and astrolabe. At the sides are hosts of angels, while on the roof is *Saint Francis* with a yoke on his shoulders that is held by the hand of God.

ALTAR
The Gothic papal altar stands at the center of the sanctuary at the top of four steps. It was consecrated by Pope Innocent IV in 1253, and it is possible to see the tomb of Saint Francis below through a small window. His body was moved there in 1230. Access to the actual tomb was through a narrow tunnel, visited in 1449 by Pope Nicholas V and then by Sixtus IV, who however had the entrance walled up in 1476.
The altar table, a large marble monolith donated by John of Brienne (a Byzantine emperor) in the 13th century, rested on four large slabs of red stone from Subasio and twenty colonnettes and arches decorated with mosaics.

APSE: the *Celestial Glory* or the message of Francis to his followers for a new Church (now, however, the *Last Judgement* is there)

The apse vault as narrated by Giorgio Vasari and Brother Ludovico da Pietralunga, was frescoed until the 17th century with scenes of *Saint Francis in Glory and the Mission Entrusted by the Saint to the Minorites,* painted by Stefano Fiorentino, a pupil of Giotto. Because the frescoes were so deteriorated and difficult to interpret, Cesare Sermei, at the time the best known artist in Assisi, was called in to replace them. Since the frescoes by Stefano Fiorentino were destroyed when they were replaced by Sermei's Last Judgement of 1623, his work has been sharply criticized. Only recently has he been given credit for his attempt to give pictorial movement and light to the dark apse conch where the 14th century decoration was beyond repair. By using sky blue, he created an effect of opening up the wall and his brilliant colors were part of this attempt to harmonize his style with that of the Giottesque vault sections.

CHOIR STALLS

The choir stalls behind the altar were finished in 1471 (to which the signature on the right end bears witness). Two orders of stalls and back rests are carved with leaves and fantastic figures. The work was begun in 1467 by Umbrian woodworkers, such as Crispolto di Polto and Polimante della Spina, and was then finished by Apollonio Petrocchi da Ripatransone and Tommaso d'Antonio Fiorentino. Tommaso was bound to the artistic ateliers of the Tuscan city and, perhaps in the same way, to the popularity in Assisi of Florentine painting in the time of Lorenzo the Magnificent.

Apse zone, wooden choir stalls and fresco of the *Last Judgement* by Cesare Sermei

SOUTH or LEFT TRANSEPT: *Stories of the Passion of Christ*

The south arm of the transept is covered by a spacious barrel vault and has a Chapel to Saint John the Baptist at the head. A superb cycle of frescoes decorates this space, the basic theme of which is the parallelism between the lives of Francis and Christ, with the narration of the *Stories of the Passion.* As early as Cavalcaselle's studies of 1864 (who dated them to 1320) the execution was attributed to the Sienese painter Pietro Lorenzetti who would have replaced Giotto and his pupils, perhaps because of his skill, at the beginning of the 14th century. Giorgio Vasari however mentioned Giotto, Puccio Capanna and Pietro Cavallini and also indicated Walter VI of Brienne, titular duke of Athens (lord for a certain period of Florence who then moved to Lecce), as the patron.

It is generally believed that Pietro Lorenzetti started working in the chapel of Saint John the Baptist and then continued, with a change in his artistic style, on the transept surfaces. This variation has been the source of bitter arguments among art historians because practically everyone was aware of the change in style and quality. Carlo Volpe, the greatest Lorenzetti scholar, attempted to explain these different 'modes'. Around 1310, probably in line with the Angevin patronage, there was a period in which the finest Sienese painters of

View of the presbytery and the south transept

the time, such as Simone Martini and the Lorenzetti, were working in Assisi. Volpe agrees with Cavalcaselle in assigning most of Pietro Lorenzetti's decoration in the south transept to 1320. The less successful of these six scenes of the *Passion before the Death of Christ* (even called "aberrations" by some) are assigned to a slightly earlier period, characterized by a certain artistic immaturity. Yet there are also those who consider them particularly well painted. Other art historians, including Pietro Toesca, propose an early phase between 1335 and 1335, followed by a second dating to between 1339 and 1340. Lorenzetti, according to Volpe, generally worked alone, without a workshop, and was helped only by his brother Ambrogio. Their artistic itinerary has much in common. Volpe's dates are generally accepted by current art historians, except for those who believe that the Chapel of John the Baptist was not built until after 1340.

Chapel of San Giovanni Battista

According to Vasari, the Chapel of Saint John the Baptist, and that of Saint Nicholas in the north transept, were designed structurally by Agnolo and Agostino Senesi (although Carlo Volpe finds this unlikely). Art historians however disagree as to the dates. The chapel, like that of Saint Nicholas, is generally referred to the years

South transept, Pietro Lorenzetti, so-called *Sunset Madonna*

South transept, Pietro Lorenzetti, so-called *Sunset Madonna*, detail with *Saint Francis*

around the turn of the century when, after the building of the transept, Angevin commissions were being carried out in the basilica. It has however been noted that in a description of a visit to the Basilica around 1340, no mention is made of the Chapel, which would accordingly have been built at a later date. This in turn would influence the dating of Pietro Lorenzetti's original frescoes. A testament of 1300 does mention an altar of Saint John the Baptist, but it may not actually have been this chapel. Those who propose a date of around 1300 for the Chapel, believe it was commissioned by Cardinal Napoleone Orsini for his own tomb (never used) in parallel to the Chapel of Saint Nicholas (in the north transept) which he had made for his brother, Cardinal Gaetano Orsini, who died in the conclave of 1292-1294. A reconstruction of this sort would seem to be corroborated by the presence of the Orsini armorial bearings on the stained glass windows of the chapel. Moreover, Napoleone was a friend of the bishop of Arezzo, Guido Tarlati, who commissioned works from Pietro Lorenzetti, and explains the artist's presence in Assisi. The dating, according to Volpe, would then be between 1210 and 1215.

Most of these are however suppositions for the pictorial decoration of the Chapel has in great part been lost, except for a trompe l'oeil triptych over the altar with the *Madonna and Child between Saint John the Baptist and Saint Francis*. This fresco is unanimously considered, as far back as Cavalcaselle, to be earlier than the scenes frescoed by Lorenzetti on the vaults of the transept. It is known as the *Sunset Madonna*, because it is illuminated by the rays of the setting sun. According to Carlo Volpe this picture presents us with the first encounter of the young Lorenzetti with the art of Giotto. Below the painted triptych are panels decorated with heraldic emblems and, on the right, the effigy of the patron. Vasari mentioned the duke of Athens, Angevin vicar of Florence in 1326 and Lord of the city in 1342, Walter VI of Brienne, whose crest, the rampant lion, is in one of the shields (but Supino has rejected this attribution and Carlo Volpe too is doubtful).

The relic of the Veil of the Madonna (donated in 1414) is preserved in the chapel. It was carried in procession through the streets of Assisi in a particularly evocative ceremony.

The frescoes in the transept

The only real damage suffered by Lorenzetti's frescoes in the transept was the result of the construction of an altar, in the 16th century, at the foot of the *Crucifixion*. In 1963 the frescoes were however radically restored and various parts were considerably modified. The scenes were drastically cleaned to remove the molds and dust and much of the 14th century retouching in *fresco secco* came away with the water. At the time these frescoes were not considered particularly important and fewer precautions were taken than with others, since restoration work was closely dependent on art historical criticism. It is therefore now even more difficult to interpret the cycle and attempt attributions.

The frescoes of uncertain paternity, which Carlo Volpe attributes to Lorenzetti when he had not yet achieved full artistic maturity, are

South transept, view of the vault

the six in the transept vaulting. It should however be noted that if the work really was done in 1320, the artist at the time was about forty years old (and therefore fully mature).

The cycle begins with the upper part of the vault, at the center.

In the scene of the *Entry of Christ into Jerusalem*, the quality is exceedingly high, especially in the rendering of the buildings in the background, with the shadows on the walls of the palace at the center and, on the right, the representation of the city gates in a decorative panel of classic taste. According to many historians, with the

South transept, Pietro Lorenzetti, *Last Supper*

exception of Volpe, the scene is not by Pietro but perhaps by his brother Ambrogio.

In the panel of the *Last Supper*, the scene takes place inside a room shown in perspective, with illumination which contrasts with the dark outer world (on the left, above, the moon and stars). The circular arrangement of the figures calls to mind Byzantine representations of the Palaeologian period, while the scene at the side, with the figures busy in the kitchen and the dog and rooster, are typically Gothic in their inclusion of genre (making the story more alive and relevant). Many, but once again not Carlo Volpe, believe it to have been done by Pietro Lorenzetti's collaborators and not by the artist himself.

The *Washing of the Feet* has been acknowledged as one of the most intense scenes in the cycle and is definitely thought to be by Pietro Lorenzetti himself. Great care has been taken in depicting the details: note the decorations with pelicans in the spandrels of the arcades. Once more there is the contrast between the illumination of the room and the exterior darkness.

This scene too, contrary to Volpe's attribution, is considered by many to have been painted by Ambrogio Lorenzetti.

South transept, Pietro Lorenzetti, the *Washing of Feet* and below, the *Capture of Christ*

In the panel of the *Capture of Christ in the Garden,* one of the scenes damaged most in the 1960s restoration, Pietro Lorenzetti depicts the emotion of the event through the poses of the figures who seem to fold themselves around Christ who remains unmoved. There is a wonderful night scene in the background with the moon and stars. This scene too, with the exception of Volpe, is attributed by many to Pietro Lorenzetti.

In the *Flagellation* the artist expresses his inventiveness in the dynamic poses of the group of figures in the center and the position of Christ, whose soft line acts as counterpoint to the scourger next to him. Once more a night scene outside and, once more the presence of a genre scene with the runaway monkey on the rooftops and the owners still at the window below. The face of Pilate is particularly intense, bearded as are the pagans, but with a laurel wreath on his head, perhaps in reference to Frederick II. To be noted is the great care taken in depicting the architectural space and the ornamentation with lions and putti. The scene takes place inside the Palace of Pilate (or of the Proconsul) on the basis of an iconographic scheme that had by this time become standard and had been used by the Sienese painter Agostino di Duccio with whom Lorenzetti had studied (but this iconography also continues into the 15th century with few variations even in Piero della Francesca's famous *Flagellation* in Urbino). The scene, once more with the exception of Volpe, is to be attributed to Pietro's brother Ambrogio or assistants.

In the panel of the *Way to Calvary*, Lorenzetti has paid particular attention to the depiction of the urban setting. Jerusalem is shown in the background, enclosed in its powerful walls which, in the front, consist of imposing substructures like pylons with small barrel vaults (substructures used in the 15th century to articulate the facade overlooking the valley of the Sacro Convento). The drama of the event and the suffering of Christ are invariably shown not only by the arch of his body but also by that of the figures near him and the Madonna. Many, except for Carlo Volpe, do not attribute the scene to Pietro Lorenzetti.

The frescoes unanimously attributed to Pietro Lorenzetti are those of the *Crucifixion* and the events that follow Christ's death.

The fresco of the *Crucifixion* is the largest of all and occupies the space of four panels of the vault. Art historians are unanimous in considering this the high point of Lorenzetti's oeuvre, in particular because of the freedom and the "narrative power" of the sixty-five figures shown at the foot of the Cross. Carlo Volpe, moreover, noted the innovative treatment of the iconography with the insertion of the three crosses within one fresco. This concept was later to

South transept, Pietro Lorenzetti, *Crucifixion*

be very popular in Umbrian and Sienese painting. The large lacuna in the lower center is due to an altar which was added in the 16th century and then removed.

The location of the picture of the *Deposition from the Cross* is inverted in its reading with respect to the direction so far followed in the succession of scenes of the *Life of Christ* (no longer from top to bottom, but the other way around, just as Giotto had done in the Chapel of the Magdalene). Volpe considers this fresco to be entirely by Lorenzetti, even though fully aware of and influenced by Giotto. The line of *Christ's* body at the center of the scene is highly dynamic, and all the figures are gathered together in a single arch. The geometric dialogue between the shape of Christ and that of the *pious woman* bending down to kiss his feet, in a sort of symmetry which cuts through the compositional arch, is of great interest.

In the panel with the *Entombment*, Lorenzetti focussed on the heart-rending anguish of the *pious women* in the background, hands raised in grief, while the figure of *Mary* seems to merge with the body of *Christ*.

In the *Resurrection*, his use of perspective permits Lorenzetti to greatly dilate the narrow surface available, inserting a barren landscape above , while in the wider lower part the central axis is accentuated by the figure of *Christ*, framed by *Angels*. The sleeping *soldiers* below are also rendered with highly innovative and interesting foreshortening.

For many scholars Lorenzetti's inventiveness diminished in the panel with the *Descent of Christ to Hell (Harrowing of Hell),* despite the fact that the meeting of the hand of Christ and that of the old *Adam* is a highly charged emotional moment.

Lorenzetti painted the scene of the *Stigmata of Francis* on the entrance staircase to the convent, a salient event in the identification of *Francis* with *Christ* (here shown instead of the Seraph) and the underlying motive behind the entire evangelical cycle in the transept. Lorenzetti's reference to Giotto in the landscapes is evident.

Lower sacristy
The room is first documented in 1341 but it must have been built as early as the end of the 13th century, together with the other side chapels of the lower church. In 1952 a fire revealed a fresco painted by the Giottesque Figline Master, in the second decade of the 14th century, with a *Madonna and Child, Saint Francis and Saint Clare.* In this work too the Master shows his acquaintance with Giotto's work in Santa Croce in Florence, but adds an accentuated precision and elegance which ties him in with the Gothic taste of the Anjou.

Hidden sacristy or Campanile (bell tower)
The so-called hidden Sacristy was set into the lower part of the old 13th century bell tower after it was built, reinforcing the corner structures for the insertion of the cross vault. The cupboards against the walls date to 1622 and were carved by a certain Master Stefano. The bell tower is generally described as having been built in 1239 on the basis of an inscription on the bronze bells (but the date would refer to the casting of the bells and not to the construction of the bell tower). The masonry stratification still visible indicates that it was later than the circular tower nearby. It is also lined up with the large pylon buttresses which characterize the side walls of the basilica, so that it was apparently built together with them and also served as buttress.

NORTH or RIGHT TRANSEPT: *Stories of the Childhood of Christ*

The *Madonna Enthroned with the Child Jesus Blessing Saint Francis*
is in the second register above the entrance to the Chapel of the
Magdalene.
This is one of the few fragments of what is thought to have been a
large pictorial program painted by Cimabue on the walls of the
transept. The attribution to the Florentine master has also been
based on stylistic features, and on the whole this is generally accepted. The figures seem to show several distinctive features of
Cimabue's style, such as the perfectly oval faces, the long slightly
aquiline nose, the eyes set close together and the ring curls framing
the face and falling on the shoulders. The three locks in particular
which project from the compact mass of the features of the *Angels*
has been thought of as a sort of signature motif for Cimabue, for
they also appear in the *Angels* surrounding the *Dying Christ* in the
Crucifixion in the south-east transept. The large areas of repainting,
done over the centuries, do not alter the value of Cimabue's art. The
Virgin is seated on a wooden throne with *Saint Francis* on the right
(on her left). The barefoot *Francis* holds a closed book and has a
very thoughtful expression. The treatment is extremely realistic
(note the stigmata). There may have been another saint, on the left,
to make the composition symmetrical, but the figure was lost when
this picture was included in the new layout of the architectural cor-
nices which articulate the walls. The halo which overlaps the upper
cornice at the top also bears witness to the difficulties encountered

North transept, general view

North transept, Cimabue, *Madonna and Child in Majesty*

in adapting the *Maestà* to this new subdivision of areas. Cimabue may have painted this picture in the early 1280s and during his time achieved great fame and served as model for various contemporary artists.

Below the *Maestà* are five *Blessed Franciscans in Adoration* (the one in the center is frontal, those at the side in profile) which must have been part of the decoration of a 14th century altar. They were attributed to Pietro Lorenzetti by F. M. Perkins in 1908.

To the left of the *Maestà* is the *Crucifixion,* attributed to Giotto or his highly gifted pupils under his direction.
The scene is highly agitated with *Angels* moving around the Cross in all directions. On the left the group of grieving figures who were there when it happened stands out, with the fainting *Madonna* and the *Marys* (note the woman in the background raising her arms in desperation). On the right are the *Franciscan friars* in adoration, a reference to the relevance of the Death of Christ despite the passing of centuries.

Above, beginning with the third register, are a series of panels with

North transept, Giotto, *Crucifixion*

the *Stories of the Childhood of Christ* painted by Giotto's collaborators under his direction. They form one of the masterpieces of Italian 14th century painting. The so-called Master of San Nicola certainly worked on these, but another painter ("Giotto's Relative" or probably Stefano Fiorentino) was also present, marked by the elegance of sfumato effects, with soft transparent shadows, closer to Gothic modes.

The *Annunciation* on the inner facade was painted by one of Giotto's assistants. The figures of the *Angel* and of *Mary* have been distanced from the opening of the chapel of San Nicola. After this scene was finished, the workshop stopped for a while. The painting has been attributed to the Master of San Nicola, who had also begun to work on the scenes of the miracles of Saint Francis.

The *Visitation of Mary and Elisabeth*, attributed to Giotto, is on the vaulting. It has been noted that with respect to the corresponding scene in Padua, here Giotto approached the problem of representing architecture in foreshortening.

The *Nativity* scene, attributed by many to Giotto himself, is at the center of the vault. Various details taken from the apocryphal Gospels have also been included in the story, such as the *melancholy*

North transept, general view of the Giottesque vault

Saint Joseph, who never appears in this form in the stories officially accepted by the Church.

In the panel on the right wall, above the *Crucifixion,* in the third register, is the *Epiphany* or *Adoration of the Magi.* The great popularity enjoyed by this scene among early 14th century Umbrian painters can be attributed to the quest for physical beauty expressed in the figures and the attentive choice of colors.

The *Presentation of Jesus in the Temple,* attributed to Giotto, is shown in the panel of the third register on the left. The scene takes place in an architectural ambience consisting of a Gothic church

North transept, Giotto, *Nativity*

supported by piers, set therefore in Giotto's time. The figures are adapted to the structure (and not vice versa) as shown by the half-hidden *Saint Joseph*.

On the vault, at the left, is the *Massacre of the Innocents* in which the influence of Gothic realism is particularly evident. The rendering of the desperation of the *women*, on the right, is shown with masterly skill, while the bodies of the innocent *babes* are piled up at the center.

The *Flight to Egypt* is in the next panel, on the left wall. *Mary* is shown riding her ass through a harsh landscape where the palm, symbol of peace, bends as she passes.

In the *Christ among the Doctors*, the Temple of Jerusalem is depicted as the nave of a Gothic basilica to bring the event into the present time. This is one of the most skillful forerunners of the one-point perspective which was developed in the 15th century.

In the third register on the left, interrupted by the entrance to the cloister outside, is *Jesus Leaving the City of Jerusalem and Returning to Nazareth*. The warm rosy tones of the city, which looks like a western Gothic town, give us an idea of what an Italian city looked like in the Middle Ages.

The scenes frescoed on the walls in the second register, along the line of the *Maestà* and the *Crucifixion*, depict some of the best

North transept, Giotto, *Massacre of the Innocents*

North transept, Giotto, *Christ among the Doctors*

known miracles of Saint Francis and children. There is the *Boy of Suessa Taken out of the Ruins of a House* (note the perspective rendering of the building and the arched movement of the weeping women) and the *Boy of Suessa Resuscitated by Saint Francis*. The

North transept, Giotto, *Boy of Suessa Taken from the Ruins of his House*

scene takes place inside a room shown with great perspective skill, with particular attention paid to the decoration in various materials. Both these scenes have been attributed to Giotto, or a highly gifted collaborator, the Master of San Nicola, who surely began them. They were probably finished in the lower parts, after the interruption of the work yard, by a pupil of Giotto's of Florentine origin (called "Relative of Giotto" by Previtali) who with respect to his Master tended to overcome the close set layout of the figures for an attention to decorative details that was much more Gothic.

On the left wall, near the stairs leading to the cloister above, on the right is a scene with *Saint Francis and Death*, in which the figure of the saint is highly realistic. On the left is the *Miracle of a Child who was Unhurt after Falling from the Top of a House.*

Next to the entrance to the Chapel of San Nicola are five saints, *Francis, Elizabeth of Hungary, Margaret, Henry of Hungary, Louis of Toulouse*, painted by Simone Martini. Henry and Margaret were members of the Anjou family. The *Madonna and Child between Saint Stephen and Saint Ladislas*, in the back corner, was also painted by Simone Martini for King Charles Robert (Carobert) of Hungary. The iconographic program is thus basically Angevin-Hungarian, to celebrate the sanctity of the ruling house, where, immediately after her death, Saint Elisabeth was taken as an example for the

North transept, Giotto, *Boy of Suessa Brought Back to Life*

Franciscan Tertiaries. The dating oscillates, in general, between 1317 and 1323 (although not all agree on this point) while there seem no doubts that they are by Simone Martini.

North transept, Giotto and pupils, *Miracle of a Child who was Unhurt after Falling from the Top of a House*

North transept, Simone Martini, *Saints Francis, Louis of Toulouse, Elizabeth of Hungary, Clare and Elzeario*

North transept, Simone Martini, *Madonna and Child between Saints Stephen and Ladislas*

Chapel of San Nicola

The Chapel of Saint Nicholas opens in the back wall, north of the transept. It was built by Cardinal Napoleone Orsini in memory of his brother Gian (Giovanni) Gaetano, who died during the conclave of 1292-1294. Some art historians, though, prefer to assign it to Angevin patronage, one branch of which had taken Saint Nicholas as their patron saint (Balkan saint par excellence, a sign of the eastern 'vocation' by the southern branch of the family). Vasari says that the Chapel, as well as that of Saint John the Baptist across from it in the south transept, was built by Agostino and Agnolo Senesi, around 1300. Currently however the opinion is that the decoration of the walls, prior to 1306, seems to indicate that the chapel was built at the turn of the century. It resembles the chapel of Saint John the Baptist in the southern transept, a polygonal vaulted chapel with a vestibule covered by a barrel vault. Giottesque painters, who had collaborated with the workshop on the last scenes of the Franciscan cycle in the upper church, frescoed the chapel with the *Stories of Saint Nicholas*, the figures of the Apostles and

Saints, almost literally adopting some of these motifs. For some art historians these scenes form a time limit (by 1306) for the termination of the Giottesque cycle in the upper church as well. At least two Giottesque painters seem to have been at work on the pictorial decoration of the Chapel of Saint Nicholas: the Expressionist Master who did the portraits of the two Orsini brothers and most of the inner facade, and a second painter, known as the Master of San Nicola (Previtali), who did most of the scenes. The level of execution in these is so high that he has been identified with Giotto himself, while some consider him a pupil, later also active in the transept with the episodes

North transept, interior of the Chapel of San Nicola

North transept, Chapel of San Nicola, Palmerino di Guido,
Saint Nicholas Saving Three Innocents

of the *Resurrection of the Boy of Suessa*. Then there are others who identify the Master of San Nicola with the Expressionist Master. Pietro Toesca believes that there was a third painter, active above all in the triptych frescoed on the tomb, on the back wall.

In the barrel vault, from top to bottom, *Saint Nicholas Giving the Maidens of Pantera a Dowry* (throwing three golden balls or rods) The perspective rendering of the room is particularly successful. *Saint Nicholas Saving some Sailors from a Storm* (lost scene).

Saint Nicholas Receiving Three Roman Knights in Myra or *Blessing a penitent with a rope around his neck who is kneeling before him*. The use of brilliant colors, on the garments, makes this scene particularly lively; note also the fine cathedral shown in the background.

Next come two *Apostles*.

On the barrel vault, on the left, *Saint Nicholas Saving Three Innocents from Decapitation*. In this case too the attention paid to the perspective seems to indicate the circle of Giotto, or even the hypothesis that Giotto supervised the execution of the entire cycle. *Sailors Pouring the Oil Dedicated to Diana into the Sea; Saint Nicholas Appearing to Constantine in a Dream*. Next come two *Apostles*.

On the side walls the miracles of the Saint continue with on the right *Saint Nicholas Bringing a Child Back to Life, Saint Nicholas Freeing the Slave Adeodatus, Saint Nicholas Returning Adeodatus to his Parents*.

Only one scene remains on the left wall: *An Elderly Jew Striking the Image of the Saint*.

Above the entrance arch, on the inner facade, are *Saint Francis and*

Saint Nicholas Presenting Giovanni Gaetano and Napoleone Orsini to Christ, shown blessing within a shrine. These figures were however added later than the neighboring scenes (leading to a suspicion that the Chapel may have been rededicated or at least that the initial program was changed).

On the back wall is the *tomb of Giovanni Gaetano Orsini,* who died in 1292 but was not brought here until 1296. The tomb was made in the early 14th century by a Ro-

North transept, Chapel of San Nicola, Palmerino di Guido, *An Elderly Jew Striking the Image of the Saint*

man sculptor whose style is close to that of Arnolfo di Cambio. Above the tomb is a painted triptych with the *Madonna and Child* at the center. This illusionistic attempt to depict an altarpiece in fresco is rather unusual.

The three stained-glass two-light windows contain figures of sixteen *Saints* of Giottesque school. Here, for the first time in Italian art, the problem of the relationship between painters and master glass workers comes to the fore. In other words that of the artist who designed the windows and perhaps made the glass, and of those who cut and mounted the pieces (precisely following indications or, perhaps, making mistakes, or modifying the original instructions). This is particularly important here because Giotto then may have designed, but not executed, the stained glass. For a long time, after Giovanni Marchini's studies, it was believed that the two roles coincided and that most of the stained-glass windows in the lower church, including those in the Chapel of Saint Nicholas, were by Giovanni di Bonino, the so-called Figline Master. Recently however this identity has been refuted and the hypothesis has been newly broached that Giotto designed, but did not make, the windows (for the Chapel of San Martino, by Simone Martini; for the others, by Lorenzetti).

North transept, Chapel of San Nicola, Tomb of Giovanni Orsini

D) THE CHAPELS ON THE RIGHT SIDE

Chapel of Santa Maria Maddalena
The back wall of this square chapel dedicated to Saint Mary Magdalene and with a cross vault is practically entirely taken up by a large window, below which are marble slabs with mosaic decoration from the old iconostasis (the partition which separated the friar's part of the nave from that of the pilgrims).
Some art historians believe that after 1305, when the cycle in Padua in the Scrovegni Chapel had been completed, the bishop of Assisi, Teobaldo Pontano, commissioned the frescoes in the Chapel of the

Chapel of Santa Maria Maddalena, Giotto, *The Saint with Teobaldo Pontano, the Donor*

Magdalene with episodes from the *Life of the Saint* from Giotto. This is probably the oldest cycle dedicated to her and is based on Jacobus de Voragine's *Golden Legend* (a famous text in the Middle Ages). Giotto's presence in the city in 1309 has been tied in with this commission. The stylistic features here are similar to those in

Chapel of Santa Maria Maddalena, Giotto, *Supper in the House of the Pharisee*

the Padua frescoes: the same soft modeling of the forms and the same use of color - blues and reds, pinks and violet grays - with carefully studied passages of light to shade and a monumentality of the ensemble. These features were later developed by Giotto in the frescoes in the Peruzzi Chapel in Florence. While the Master had numerous assistants (the so-called Giottesque painters) in Assisi, the scene of the *Ecstasy of the Magdalene* and the portrait of *Teobaldo Pontano Adoring Saint Rufinus and the Magdalene* have been attributed to Giotto himself. The Cosmatesque columns, for instance, are carefully rendered and betray the artist's interest in the architectural settings. The hand of the Giottesque Expressionist Master has been identified in many parts of the *Supper in the House of the Pharisee* and the *Landing in Marseilles of the Magdalene*.

The *Magdalene* cycle on the walls begins in the lower register of the wall to the left of the entrance, and continues on the right wall and then the lunette.

To be noted on the left: the portrait of *Teobaldo Pontano*.

Supper of Christ and Magdalene in the House of the Pharisee.

The *Raising of Lazarus* is undoubtedly one of the finest scenes, and is assigned to Giotto, for the style is close to that of the Scrovegni Chapel in Padua. Giotto's mature style here achieves one of its highest points, with color treated with great attention. Even the shadows are no longer a simple chiaroscuro. *Transportation of Magdalene to Heaven.*

Chapel of Santa Maria Maddalena, Giotto, *Noli me tangere*

Chapel of Santa Maria Maddalena, Giotto, *Journey of Saint Mary Magdalene to Marseilles*

On the right wall: the *"Noli me tangere"*, a scene very close to the analogous scene in Padua.

The *Journey of Saint Mary Magdalene to Marseilles*. There is a fine perspective on the right, beyond the lighthouse, while scenes of daily life are shown near the boats.

Mary Magdalene Speaking with the Angels. Mary Magdalene Receiving the Vestments from the Hermit Zosimus
The stained-glass windows of the chapel are of particular note and are close in style to those in the upper church, in particular the panels in the quadrifore of the south transept, a Gothic work by masters from across the Alps, to which the general layout as well as the depictions of flowers, vines and naturalistic leaves framing the scenes or figures bear witness.

Vestibule between the buttresses or Chapel of San Valentino
The Chapel of San Valentino was dedicated to the saint before 1388, ten years after Blessed Valentine from Narni, who is painted on one of the piers, died on Monte Subasio. The coat of arms of the Fiumi counts on the vault dates to the 17th century.

Chapel of Sant'Antonio da Padova
The chapel of Saint Anthony was built before the 14th century, and belonged to a family in Assisi until it passed to the Montefeltro of Urbino in 1429. Square in plan, it is covered by a cross vault which has unusual round moldings on the ribbing dating to 1487. The frescoes with the *Stories of Saint Anthony of Padua* date to 1610 and are by Cesare Sermei. On the left wall, in the lunette, is *Saint Anthony Preaching before Gregory IX*. Further down *Saint Anthony Healing a Woman* and then *Apparition of Saint Anthony to the Money Lenders*. On the right wall, in the lunette, is the *Miracle of Saint*

View of the entrance to the Chapel of Sant'Antonio da Padova

Anthony in Rimini where he makes a mule kneel before the Sacrament, below *Saint Anthony Returning a Man to Life* and *Saint Anthony and Brother Elias before Gregory IX.*
On the inner facade is *Saint Anthony Returning a Young Man to Life and Saving a Shipwreck Victim,* while in the soffits of the entrance

Chapel of Sant'Antonio, Giovanni di Bonino, stained glass window

arch and on the window splays are busts of *Saints* and *Franciscans*. The stained glass, which illustrates episodes from the life of the Saint, has been variously assigned to Giottesque masters or to Giovanni di Bonino. It was certainly made prior to 1317.

Chapel of Santo Stefano, stained glass on a cartoon attributed to Simone Martini

Vestibule between the buttresses or Chapel of San Lorenzo

In the narrow passage between the Chapels of Saint Anthony and of Saint Stephen, used in its turn as a Chapel and dedicated to Saint Lawrence, are frescoes that were probably painted by Andrea de' Bartoli da Bologna, in 1368. On the curved surfaces of the buttress turret is the *Martyrdom of Saint Lawrence*, while on the walls are the *Capture of Christ* (on the right) and the *Agony in the Garden* (left).

Chapel of Santo Stefano

Like the ones at the sides, the chapel was built at the end of the 13th century, and was then renovated in subsequent centuries. It is square in plan and has a cross vault with a large four light window in the back wall. Turned over in 1535 to the Confraternity of Saint Stephen, in 1574 the Confraternity commissioned Dono Doni, a painter from Assisi, to paint episodes from the *Life of the Saint* on the walls. (Doni died the year after and the works were carried out by his pupils as well as by Giacomo Giorgetti in the middle of the 17th century).

In the cross vaulting are *Sibyls* associated with various *Prophets*.

In the lunettes are scenes by Doni dealing with Saint Stephen. From the right, *Saint Stephen's Debate in the Synagogue*, then *Saint Stephen Driven from Jerusalem* on the inner facade and the *Stoning of Saint Stephen* on the left.

The stained-glass window in the quadrifore, according to some, was done on a cartoon by Simone Martini, but others believe it to be by Angioletto da Gubbio. References to the Angevin milieu appear in some of the other scenes, such as *Saint Louis King*, since the Chapel was dedicated to Saint Louis of Tolouse, and the scene of *Cardinal Gentile Partino da Montefiore*, who commissioned the stained-glass windows after 1312.

E) THE CHAPELS ON THE LEFT SIDE

Chapel of San Martino

In 1312 Cardinal Gentile Partino da Montefiore, closely connected to the House of Anjou, ordered this Chapel dedicated to Saint Martin to be built, generously supplying funds. Work however went on slowly and it was not until 1315 that the Figline Master made the stained-glass window. The fresco decoration on the walls, about which we have no certain information but which was assigned by Cavalcaselle to Simone Martini, was painted between 1317 and 1320. Vasari assigns the paintings in this Chapel to Puccio Capanna, but by the 18th century art historians tended to ascribe them to Simone Martini. For decades the date

View of the entrance to the Chapel of San Martino

has also been a moot question: some say 1315-1317, some 1320, some 1324-1326, some 1328-1333, and some 1330-1335. At present critics prefer the earlier date of 1315-1317.

If these scenes are really by Simone Martini, he was certainly called in because of his activity at the Neapolitan court of Robert of Anjou, where his work had been characterized by a typical Angevin Gothic taste, especially in the dynamic outlines of the figures, in line with French painting of the time. In these paintings in Assisi the painter created one of the masterworks of 14th century paint-

Chapel of San Martino, intrados of the arch, Simone Martini, *Saint Anthony and Saint Francis*

ing, in a highly elegant style of great beauty. Contacts with Giotto's work are also evident but in Simone Martini's hands the stylistic elements become less grave, not as solid, with an accent on surface movement rather than depth. Simone Martini paved the way for the new generations of Sienese painters, extremely aware of techniques and materials, characterized by the richness of pattern and tooled decorative motifs, as well as by a realistic rendering of the events and the psychology of the figures.

Eight *Saints*, full figure, are shown in the soffit of the entrance arch, among which *Saint Clare, Saint Catherine, Saint Francis* and *Saint Anthony* in particular can be noted.

On the walls are the *Stories of Saint Martin*, a saint who can be compared to Francis in various episodes (in particular the episode in which *Francis is Honored by a Simple Man* and above all *Francis Giving his Cloak to a Poor Man*). The Angevin patronage, with King Robert as testamentary executor for Cardinal Gentile Partino, explains the choice of Martin, for the French saint, as Bishop of Gaul and Touraine, was the patron of the dynasty. The four pairs of *Saints* set into bifores in the soffits of the entrance arch include *Saint Louis of France* and *Saint Louis of Toulouse* as well as *Saint Francis*, and *Saint Elisabeth of Hungary* with *Saint Clare*. These were probably the last figures to be frescoed in the Chapel, for Saint Louis was canonized in 1317.

As in the Chapel of Saint Mary Magdalene, the cycle begins in the lowest register, from left to right.

Chapel of San Martino, Simone Martini, *Saint Martin Dividing his Mantle with a Poor Man*

Saint Martin Dividing his Mantle with a Poor Man at the Gates of Amiens. In 1958 the fresco was detached to avoid further deterioration, revealing numerous pentimenti and the sinopia.

Christ Appears to Saint Martin in a Dream Holding the Cloak He had Given Away. It is likely that the group on the left, with *Christ and the Angels*, was executed by an assistant. Note the love for detail in the saint's bedcover, not only in the plaid coverlet but also in the folds that model the body of Martin underneath.

Emperor Julian Knights Martin. The reality of this event is highlighted by the presence of musicians and personages who preside at the ceremony, in a close continuity between the classical and medieval worlds.

Saint Martin Renounces Arms and Confronts the Enemy Armed with a Cross. The eagles on the emperor's tent seem to point to an

Chapel of San Martino, Simone Martini, *Christ Appearing in a Dream to Saint Martin Holding the Cloak He had Given Away*

attempt at creating a parallel between Saint Francis/Saint Martin and Emperor Frederick II/Emperor Julian, while the warriors in the background, with the coat of arms of Assisi, would allude to the armed Guelphs in the city.

Saint Martin, Deep in Meditation, Is Shaken by a Cleric. The empty Gothic church is there to stress the aura of detachment and asceticism surrounding the saint.

The Miraculous Mass: while he is celebrating mass in Albenga, Angels give Martin back a tunic he had given to a beggar.

Chapel of San Martino, Simone Martini, *The Emperor Julian Knights Martin*

Saint Martin Bringing a Young Girl Back to Life at Chartres.
This is one of the scenes in which the artist most authoritatively
exhibits his skill in rendering space and his elegant use of colors and
details.
*The Emperor Valentinian Paying Homage to Saint Martin: the Mira-
cle of Fire.*
The emperor Valentinian had refused to receive the saint. A tongue
of fire began to burn under his throne, and the emperor is converted and throws himself at Martin's feet.
On the vault are: *The Dream of Saint Ambrose Predicting the Death*

Chapel of San Martino, Simone Martini, *Saint Martin Renouncing Arms in the Camp of the Emperor Julian*

of Saint Martin (or *the Meditation of Saint Martin*). Once more note how skillfully Simone Martini uses perspective in describing the Gothic church.

In the scene of the *Death of Saint Martin* the body of the saint is placed, in homage to his humble life style, on the bare ground (which ties in with the particular devotion of Saint Francis to Poverty), despite the richness of his garment.

Saint Martin's Funeral Rites.

This is one of the finest scenes in the cycle in the Chapel. The charming details and the mystical atmosphere are carried to

Chapel of San Martino, Simone Martini, *Death of Saint Martin*

extremes. Saint Ambrose celebrates the rites, while various person-
ages, accurately portrayed, accompany the event with music.
The stained-glass window at the back is commonly believed to be
by the Figline Master on a cartoon by Simone Martini.
On the inner facade *Cardinal Gentile da Montefiore Kneels before
Saint Martin.*

Chapel of San Martino, Maestro di Figline on a cartoon by Simone Martini, stained glass window, detail

Fontana Chapel
This small chamber is inserted between the buttresses which sup
port the basilica structures outside. The walls have remained bar
and inside is a 17th century wooden statue of the *Virgin Mary*.

Chapel of Sant'Andrea or of San Pietro d'Alcantara
The Chapel of Saint Andrew, set against the bell tower, was offici
ated over the centuries by various families, including one from
Assisi, the Aromatari, of which there is still a crest (a mortar and
pestle). The twenty-two bronze plaques on the walls are by the
sculptor Tommaso Gismondi and date to 1928.
Back in the main nave, one can go down into the Crypt.

CRYPT

According to an ancient tradition, already mentioned by Vasari in
the 16th century, the Franciscan complex was originally supposed to
have been three superposed churches. The lowest church, com
pletely underground, was to have housed the mortal remains of the
Saint, brought here from the Porziuncola. When the body was actu
ally brought here however, for fear of theft it was hidden in the wall
near the high altar in the lower church at the end of a tunnel that
was accessible until the end of the 15th century. Nothing was there
fore done with the third Basilica.
The exact whereabouts remained a mystery until 1818 when Pope
Pius VII announced the finding of the body and crowds flocked to
Assisi. It was then decided to dig the third church and use it as a
crypt for the complex. Two architects were called in to present their
proposals, Giuseppe Brizi from Assisi and Pasquale Belli of Rome.
With a Solomonic verdict, Belli's idea was chosen, but Brizi was
entrusted with the execution.
In 1824 the new crypt was inaugurated. Six years earlier when
attempts were being made to find the body of the saint, digging had
continued without pause for over fifty days, and so much material
was removed that many feared for the stability of the entire com
plex. The new crypt, decorated in the neo-classic style fashionable
at the time, satisfied no one, for both the upper churches were
Romanesque and Gothic in style.
Suggestions to redesign the crypt and create a place that was "poor
and humble, simple and evocative" were already being broached in
1918. In 1924, with the Franciscan Centennial around the corner

Crypt, the tomb of Saint Francis

new ideas for solutions were requested from various architects. In 1925 the project submitted by Ugo Tarchi was approved thanks to the intervention of Gustavo Giovannoni, despite opposition on the grounds of threats to the stability of the entire complex.

Periods of work alternated with periods of inaction and the crypt was finally inaugurated in 1932. Ugo Tarchi decided to give the ambience a severe neo-Romanesque aspect, in line with the requests of the Friars. The furnishing, even the lamps, were all in keeping, on the basis

Crypt, the back of the tomb
of Saint Francis

of a concept of architectural design which defined even the smallest details.

The tomb of Jacopa dei Settesoli is in the entrance vestibule where the two flights of steps begin. According to the tale of the *Life of Saint Francis* by Thomas of Celano, she had confirmed the reality of the miracle of the stigmata of the saint after Brother Elias had fallen into disgrace. The role of Jacopa was fundamental, even if in scene XXIII of the *Franciscan Legend* in the upper church the reality of the stigmata was shown as being ascertained by Saint Clare.

In the nave, at the center, is the altar beyond which, behind an iron grill, is the stone urn which contains the remains of Saint Francis.

In the niches at the sides are the remains of the first four companions of Francis; Rufino, Angelo, Masseo and Leo.

Back up at the top turn towards the right transept and from there into the Chapter Hall.

CHAPTER ROOM or Chapel of the Relics

In the northern transept, to the left of the Chapel of Saint Nicholas, is a door which leads to the Chapter Room, in the oldest wing of the monastic complex, the papal part dating to 1230-1240. The room is square in plan with groin vaulting which springs from the massive pylon at the center. One of the most interesting 14th century frescoes in Assisi is to be found here: the *Crucifixion and Saints* executed by Puccio Capanna around 1340 in which the monumentality in the works of his master, Giotto, are taken as far as they can go. Many of the pictorial 'conquests' of the Florentine Giottesque painters and of Giottino may very well owe a great deal to Puccio Capanna. The deeply human quality of his figures and the likenesses achieved reveal the skill of the artist at its best.

The room is now used as a chapel for the most precious relics of Saint Francis.

The *Rule* is the manuscript of the final authorization for the life of

Convent of San Francesco, Chapter hall, Puccio Capanna, *Crucifixion*

the Franciscan Order imposed by Pope Honorius III in 1223. This manuscript document was drawn up by Francis and the future pope, Gregory IX, and the papal seal has been affixed.

Convent of San Francesco, Chapter hall, *Benediction Given by Francis to Brother Leo*

The *tunic* is the one Francis wore: the coarse sheep's wool cloth bears witness to his ideal of extreme Poverty.

The *Benediction Given by Francis to Brother Leo* is a document dictated by Francis, in 1224, in answer to some of Leo's questions. Leo was one of the followers who, unlike the other brothers, was not sure of how he was to behave with regards to the evangelical precept of extreme Poverty. Back in the transept the staircases lead to the Chiostro Grande.

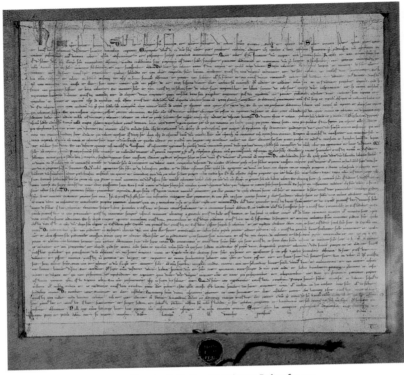

Convent of San Francesco, Chapter hall, the *Franciscan Rule of 1223*

CHIOSTRO GRANDE

The large cloister was begun in 1476, as part of the renovation of the conventual part ordered by Pope Sixtus IV. Vasari attributes the plan to Baccio Pontelli, but we know it was carried out under the supervision of the Comacine Masters. With two orders of arcading, the cloister was built as an element of closure and organization for the part of the Convent adjacent to the apse of the lower church. At the beginning of the 15th century a spring, from which water was brought to a well inside the Cloister, was still to be found next to the wall. Recent excavations have brought to light the relative structures and conduits.

The Convent as a whole was being reorganized at the time and in its structure, the Cloister mirrors an iconographic model which greatly influenced the papal court of Sixtus IV at the end of the 15th century. It was meant to call to mind the temple of Jerusalem as the citadel of Knowledge and Wisdom, harbinger of the celestial Jerusalem and in alternative, in the midst of the wild nature of Umbria, of the more worldly and political life of Rome.

Above: view of the Chiostro Grande
Below from the left: Convent of San Francesco, Chiostro Grande, a fifteenth century capital and one of the walls decorated by Dono Doni

The columns of the cloister are decorated with capitals which mirror late 15th century ornamental fashions while inside, on the lunettes, are frescoes in green earth dating to the late 15th century.

They were painted between 1564 and 1570 by Dono Doni and depict episodes from the *Stories of Saint Francis*. At present they are in a highly precarious state of conservation.

MUSEO DEL TESORO

Entrance to the Museo del Tesoro or Treasury Museum is from the Chiostro Grande. The museum is located on the upper floor of the

Convent of
San Francesco,
Museo del Tesoro,
Master of the Blue
Crucifixes, *Crucifix*

Convent of San Francesco, Museo del Tesoro, Maestro del Tesoro, *Saint Francis and four of his miracles*

cloister in the "Sala Gotica", and houses some of the works donated in the course of centuries to the basilica, including various unique examples of French 13th century goldwork.

Particular mention must be made of two altar frontals, one in embroidered yellow silk and one in red silk, made in Palermo in the 13th century and offered to the Franciscan Friars by the emperor of Byzantium, John of Brienne.

There are works by artists employed in the decoration of the walls in the complex, including sinopias, the preparatory drawings, found when the frescoes were detached (there is one by Simone Martini for the scene of *Saint Martin Sharing His Cloak with a Beggar* in the chapel of the saint, or the *Face of God* by Jacopo Torriti for his *Creation of the World* in the nave of the upper church.)

Also to be mentioned is a *Cross* by the Master of the Blue Crucifixes with the *Suffering Christ* on both sides. It was probably exhibited over the iconostasis so that it could be seen from both sides (as shown in the scene of the Christmas *Crib in Greccio* in the upper church, or, better in that of the *Verification of the Stigmata*).

A panel (antependium) with *Saint Francis surrounded by four scenes of his miracles*, painted shortly before 1253 (meant in particular to present the people with the story of the healings Francis did when alive) is of particular note. It has been assigned to an Umbrian master, known simply as the Maestro del Tesoro.

There are also any number of fine reliquaries, true masterpieces of the art of the goldsmith, as well as furnishings donated to the convent (chalices, processional crosses, candlesticks, processional banners).

Of interest too is the tabernacle, made for the lower church in the second half of the 16th century on a design by Galeazzo Alessi and dismantled by Cavalcaselle in the late 19th century because it was not 'medieval' enough.

Convent of San Francesco, Perkins Collection, Masolino da Panicale, *Madonna and Child* (15th cent.)

PERKINS COLLECTION

This important collection of Italian art, dating from the 14th to the 16th century, was given to the Sacro Convento by the American art historian Fredrick Mason Perkins (1874-1955), who spent years studying the frescoes in the upper and lower churches. These 57 works, mostly on panel, are a representative selection of the various regional schools (Umbrian, Sienese, Florentine, Venetian, Emilian). Of particular note are works by Pietro Lorenzetti, Fra Angelico, Signorelli. Number 2 is a depiction of *Francis Receiving the Stigmata* by Antoniazzo Romano of 1488: number 32, *Saint Francis* by Fra Angelico, a panel dating to around 1430; number 45 a *Saint Christopher* by Stefano di Giovanni known as Sassetta of 1440-1450; while numbers 49-53, of various religious subjects, are by Pietro Lorenzetti.

LIBRARY

The great Library of the Convent is located near the Chiostro Grande. It houses about 150,000 volumes and over a thousand manuscripts and between the 14th and 15th centuries was one of the most important in Europe. In the course of the centuries many of its treasures were taken elsewhere.

View of the Convent Library

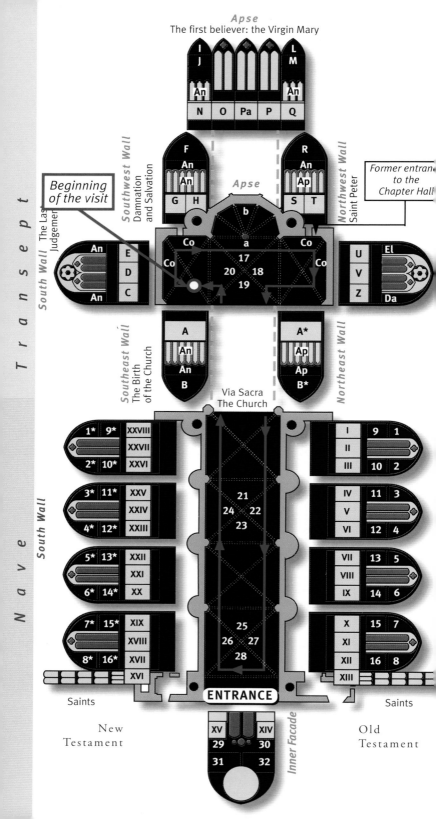

Apse
The first believer: the Virgin Mary

I J · · · L M
An · · · An
N O Pa P Q

Transept

Southwest Wall
Damnation and Salvation

F
An
An
Apse
G H

Northwest Wall
Saint Peter

R
An
Ap
S T

Former entrance
to the
Chapter Hall

South Wall The Last Judgement

An
E
D C
An

Beginning of the visit

Co · Co
a
Co · Co
17
20 · 18
19
b

U El
V
Z Da

Southeast Wall
The Birth of the Church

A
An
An
B

Northeast Wall

A*
Ap
Ap
B*

Via Sacra
The Church

Nave

South Wall

1* 9* XXVIII
XXVII
2* 10* XXVI

I 9 1
II
III 10 2

3* 11* XXV
XXIV
4* 12* XXIII

21
24 · 22
23

IV 11 3
V
VI 12 4

5* 13* XXII
XXI
6* 14* XX

VII 13 5
VIII
IX 14 6

7* 15* XIX
XVIII
8* 16* XVII

25
26 · 27
28

X 15 7
XI
XII 16 8

XVI

XIII

Saints

Saints

New
Testament

XV XIV
29 30
31 32

ENTRANCE

Inner Facade

Old
Testament

UPPER CHURCH

NORTH WALL OF NAVE

1. Creation of the World
2. Creation of Adam
3. Creation of Eve
4. Original Sin
5. Expulsion from Paradise
6. Labors of Adam and Eve
7. Sacrifice of Cain and Abel
8. Killing of Abel
9. Building of the Ark
10. Noah Entering the Ark
11. Sacrifice of Abraham
12. Visit of the Angels to Abraham
13. Isaac Blessing Jacob
14. Esau Before Isaac
15. Joseph Thrown into the Well
16. Joseph Pardons his Brothers

SOUTH WALL OF THE NAVE

1* Annunciation
2* Visitation
3* Nativity
4* Adoration of the Magi
5* Presentation in the Temple
6* Flight to Egypt
7* Dispute in the Temple
8* Baptism of Christ
9* Wedding of Cana
10* Resurrection of Lazarus
11* Taking of Christ
12* Christ before Pilate
13* Way to Calvary
14* Crucifixion
15* Lamentation over the Dead Christ
16* The Three Marys at the Sepulcher

17 Saint Luke
18 Saint Mark
19 Saint Matthew (collapsed)
20 Saint John
21 Christ the Redeemer
22 Saint John the Baptist
23 Saint Francis
24 Mary
25 Saint Gregory the Great
26 Saint Augustine
27 Saint Ambrose
28 Saint Jerome (collapsed)
29 Saint Paul
30 Saint Peter
31 Ascension
32 Pentecost
A Crucifixion
A* Crucifixion
B Christ in Glory
B* Ascent of Christ to Heaven
C Vision of the Throne
D Vision of the Angels
E Apocalyptic Christ
F Three Archangels Defeating the Dragon (Evil)
G Fall of Babylon
H Vision of Heavenly Jerusalem
I Announcement to Joachim
J Joachim Offering at the Temple
L Birth of Mary
M Marriage of the Virgin Mary
N The Virgin Mary Taking Leave from the Apostles
O Death of the Virgin Mary

P Assumption of the Virgin Mary
Q Christ and the Virgin Mary Enthroned
R God in Majesty
S Peter Healing the Lame Man
T Peter Healing the Sick
U Fall of Simon Magus
V Martyrdom of Saint Peter
Z Martyrdom of Saint Paul
a Altar
b Papal throne
An Angels
Ap Apostles
Co Wooden choir stalls
Da Da King David
El El Prophet Elijah
Pa Popes

FRANCISCAN SCENES

I Saint Francis Honored by a Simple Man
II Saint Francis Gives His Cloak to a Poor Man
III The Vision of the Palace Filled with Arms in Spoleto
IV Saint Francis Praying before the Crucifix in the Church of San Damiano
V The Renouncement of Worldly Goods
VI The Dream of Pope Innocent III
VII Pope Innocent III Approves the Franciscan Rule

VIII The Vision of the Chariot of Fire to the Friars at Rivotorto
IX The Vision of the Heavenly Thrones
X The Devils are Cast Out of Arezzo
XI Trial by Fire before the Sultan
XII The Ecstasy of Francis
XIII Nativity Scene at Greccio
XIV The Miracle of the Spring
XV The Sermon to the Birds
XVI The Death of the Knight of Celano
XVII Francis Preaches before Pope Honorius III
XVIII The Apparition of Francis to the Brothers and to Anthony
XIX Francis Receiving the Stigmata on Monte La Verna
XX The Death of Saint Francis
XXI The Apparition of Saint Francis
XXII The Confirmation of the Stigmata
XXIII The Mourning of the Poor Clares
XXIV Canonization of Saint Francis
XXV The Apparition of Francis to Gregory IX
XXVI The Immediate Healing of John of Lerida in Catalonia
XXVII The Confession of a Woman Brought Back to Life
XXVIII Saint Francis Frees Peter of Alife

THE UPPER CHURCH

The upper church is composed of a nave with a transept at the head, a cross in the form of a T in plan, that is the tau, one of Saint Francis' favorite symbols representing Salvation according to the Bible. A polygonal apse opens off the center of the transept.

The four bays of the nave are defined by composite piers, composed of clustered columns as was usual in Gothic churches, to which the weight of the large cross vaults is transferred. The structural function of the high walls is limited since the piers are the load-bearing elements. About a third of the way up, the walls are recessed to form a walkway which runs along the entire nave, rises up on the inner facade between the portal and the rose window, and passes under the trilobate arches in the arms of the transept. The space is therefore tall and soaring and full of light. Above all it is unified despite the various phases of construction and changes in plan.

The walls of the upper church are frescoed with a unified iconographic program which must be read in a given direction. Originally this reading of the walls as a sort of great Biblical, Evangelical, Franciscan and eschatological story began in the transept and was addressed to the friars of the sanctuary church or the councils who entered from the convent. The present entrance to the upper church was not built until the early 14th century, at which time the reading of the frescoes was already incomplete for the iconostasis located just before the transept obstructed the vision of the entire cycle for the pilgrims, who could see only the Franciscan stories.

When the iconostasis was removed after the Council of Trent in the second half of the 16th century, the visual continuity between nave and transept was restored, even for those who entered the upper church from the square. But the original concepts of right (the positive side) and of left (the negative, or least important side) were reversed. This is why the Franciscan stories begin in the fourth bay, and not near the present entrance, and are therefore on the observer's right, while those of *Christ* are on his left, which could originally never have been the case.

View of the Nave
Preceding page: Nave, Vault in the third bay, detail of the roundel with the *Deesis*
On pages 132-133: Upper Church, view of the Nave

To facilitate the reading, it must be kept in mind that the right-hand side for those who enter corresponds to the north wall, and the left-hand wall to the south. In order to properly read the cycle in the order that had been established when the cycle was first planned and which was to serve a didactic purpose for the pilgrims, the visitor should begin with the lower church and then climb up to the transept of the upper church. Those who enter the upper church from the facade entrance, should move up into the transept and begin their observation from the left wall near the nave (south-east wall, the direction of Jerusalem).

THE TRANSEPT

The Church as the vehicle of eternal Salvation

The transept of the upper church consists of the sanctuary or pres-bytery bay and two side bays (north and south) forming the arms of the transept. Rich ornamental bands of rinceau and geometric motifs stress the structure of the spacious cross vaults. The colors, predominantly the Angevin Gothic reds and blues, have now faded. One of the most interesting aspects of the transept decoration is the new thematic unity between the wall paintings, the ornamentation and the large stained-glass windows, of the type found in northern cathedrals.

A single iconographic program, meant to educate the religious and the pilgrims, marks the upper church, beginning with the south-eastern wall, running along the entire transept and then following the *Stories of Saint Francis* in the nave, to return to the point of departure. The transept, in particular, is devoted to depictions of themes related with the institution of the Church, since the upper church was originally the Franciscan and papal Chapter Hall. These themes then continue on the vaults of the nave (thought of as a *Via Sacra*), and the teachings of the Church in view of Salvation. Angels, which mediate between the human and divine worlds, are shown in the middle register, treated like a loggia in the south part of the transept (originally the right, because it was related to the ultraterrestrial Life). Prophets and Apostles are on the north wall of the transept (originally left).

The itinerary therefore begins with the *Crucifixion* on the southeast wall (in the direction of Jerusalem), with the death of Christ, and then with *Christ in Glory in Heaven among the Angels*, concluding the earthly life of Christ and the beginning of the story of the Church.

View of the south transept

The *Last Judgement* follows on the south wall, while the southwest wall contains scenes which refer to Damnation and Salvation. In this historical itinerary from the sacrifice of Christ to Eternal Life, the Church assumes the role of Via Sacra, that is the means of Salvation. The story of the new Church, the new People of God who

View of the north transept

take the place of the People of Israel, then begins with the *Stories* of the first believer, the Virgin Mary, to whose life the scenes in the apse are dedicated, a culminating position in the entire building. The *Stories of Saint Peter* continue in the north zone of the transept and on the north wall next to those of *Saint Paul,* the great organizer of the first Church. Lastly the story of the primitive Church and the first believers present at the foot of the Cross (shown symmetrically to those in the south transept) is synthesized on the northeast wall. At this point the *Stories of Saint Francis* begin, in perfect continuation with the stories narrated on the preceding surfaces.

SOUTH ARM OF THE TRANSEPT: Cimabue and assistants

The frescoes on the south arm of the transept were painted after those in the north transept (1265-1268), together with the vault sections of the sanctuary (1278-1280), by Cimabue and his assistants. Some art historians however suggest shifting the date of all of Cimabue's works in the transept to the late 1280s. Despite the poor state of conservation of all of these scenes – as Vasari had already noted in the 16th century, because of the alteration of the white lead used by the artist for the highlights – the monumental layout of the apocalyptic images inspired by the *Gospel according to Saint John* emerges clearly. Apocalyptic subjects of this sort were particularly important within the Franciscan Order with the Zealots, who adhered to Joachim of Fiore's theories of the coming of Doomsday.

In 1279 Pope Nicholas III condemned the extremes to which the followers of Joachim had gone, with a more tempered view of the moment of Judgment, thanks also to the explanations to be found in this cycle.

THE SOUTHEAST WALL: the *Birth of the Church of Christ*

The wall is divided into three registers, as are those in the nave, and the narration begins in the lowest register with the *Crucifixion* (A), one of the most intensely dramatic scenes of Cimabue's art, as exemplified by the shrieking *Magdalene* raising her arms to *Christ*. This is one of the most tragic depictions of the Passion of Christ in medieval art. Christ, still alive, entrusts his Mother Mary to John (the corresponding *Crucifixion* in the northern transept shows Christ already dead).

Next come the *Angels* (An, middle register) and then, above, the *Glory of Christ in Heaven* (B) to conclude his earthly life (above). If the scenes in the upper part of the nave on the left side next to the transept, with the *Annunciation* [1*] and the *Wedding in Cana* [9*], are read together with the scenes on this wall, the life of Christ is

Transept, southeast wall, Cimabue, *Crucifixion*

summed up in a brief space: the miracle of the Annunciation and His Incarnation; His fame among men after the Miracle of Cana, His Crucifixion, His Ascent to Heaven.

THE SOUTH WALL: the *Last Judgment*

Because of the large four-light window, the wall is divided into only two registers, with the *Angels* (An) on either side of the opening in the upper register. Below, the wall of the bay is subdivided into three panels, just as in the nave with the Franciscan Stories, stressing the compositional as well as theological unity. In the left scene is the *Vision of the Throne and the Book of Seven Seals* (C), where Cimabue adopts an iconography based on Byzantine models and the *Missal of Saint Michael Archangel* (to whom Saint Francis was particularly devoted as shown by the fact that he even went to Monte Gargano in Puglia). The mystical Lamb of the apocalyptic Vision has been replaced here by the Infant Jesus.

At the center is the *Vision of the Angels at the Four Corners of the Earth* [D], where Cimabue shows the four angels holding back the winds as narrated in the *Apocalypse*.

On the right, the *Apocalyptic Christ, Judge of Men* [E] surrounded

South transept, south wall, Cimabue, *Vision of the Angels*
Above: South transept, south wall, Cimabue, *Vision of the Throne*, detail

South transept, south wall, Cimabue, *Apocalyptic Christ*

by seven *Angels* with their trumpets calling the elect (among which are many Franciscans).

The large four-light opening is filled with rich stained-glass windows. In view of this extremely unified cycle, and considering the relationship with the subjects on the walls, they contain episodes from *Genesis* and the *Celebration of the Virgin*. These outstanding examples of stained glass seem to date to the late 13th century and to have been made by French masters. There are strong similarities with the stained-glass windows in the cathedral of Tours in the iconographic schemes perfected in the middle of the century at the

South transept, view of the four-light opening

court of Saint Louis IX (who sent an illuminated missal c. 1255 to Assisi). These examples help in tying this part of the basilica to the decorative apparata of the Gothic Angevin cathedrals.

THE SOUTHWEST WALL left of the apse: *Damnation and Salvation*

In the three registers on the wall are: above, in the lunette, the apocalyptic episode of the *Three Archangels Defeating the Dragon* (that is Evil) [F]; in the middle gallery (walkway)register, *Angels* [An]; in the lower register, respectively, on the left the *Fall of Babylon* [G] (the city thought of as the center of evil and corruption; note that it is shown on the left hand side of the observer) while, on the right (the part of the Just) is the *Vision of Heavenly Jerusalem of Saint John in Patmos* [H], the new homeland for those who have been judged positively by Christ at the end of time.

Cimabue touches one of the summits of his art in the *Fall of Babylon*: the *Angel* announces in heaven the damnation of the city of sin and immediately, as described in the *Book of the Apocalypse*, the buildings fall like castles of cards and the sinners and unclean beasts flee in fear as in a new Sodom and Gomorrah.

South transept, southwest wall, Cimabue, *Fall of Babylon*

View of the apse area

SANCTUARY: Cimabue and his assistants

THE APSE: and scenes from the *Life of the Virgin Mary*, the first believer of the New Church

Scenes from the *Life of the Virgin Mary*, the first believer and founder of the Church, are frescoed on the walls of the polygonal apse. Various parts of the fresco show that initially the cycle had been entrusted to masters from across the Alps who worked in a Gothic Angevin style. Subsequently the patrons chose an artist influenced by a return to the classic culture, and generally identified with Cimabue. The figures are placed so as to create a monumental composition. In his rendering of spatial depth, Cimabue still uses methods found in contemporary Byzantine painting (sloping ground lines, figures arranged in a circle, slanted biers or sheets, superposition of figures of diminishing size) and in early Christian mosaics.

The apse too is divided into three registers, and the middle register separates the *Stories of the Childhood of Mary* from those following the *Death of Christ.*

Above, beginning with the scene on the left, the story begins with the *Announcement to Joachim* [I]. Next, below, comes the *Joachim's Offering at the Temple* [J]. To the right of the large three-light window in the apse, above is the *Birth of Mary* [L]. Below the *Marriage of the Virgin Mary* [M].

Below the middle register with *Angels* [An] in the loggia gallery, are four panels with evangelical subjects related to the Virgin Mary, in this case subsequent to the death of Christ. These panels are in turn divided, at the center, on the axis of the Basilica, by two images of *Popes* (apparently *Gregory IX* on the left and *Innocent IV* on the right).

The scenes depict, on the left, the *Virgin Mary Taking Leave From the Apostles* [N], where the space of the room, as in contemporary

Apse, Cimabue, Assumption of the *Virgin Mary*

Apse, Cimabue, *Christ and Mary Enthroned*

Byzantine realism, is shown by the circular placing of the Apostles around the bed of Mary. Left, standing, John announces the death of the Virgin.

Then comes the *Dormition of the Virgin* [O], where Cimabue has depicted a three-dimensional space by superposing the figures and the death bed. Behind the bed is Christ who, with the angels and Patriarchs, receives the Virgin.

Then comes the *Assumption of the Virgin Mary in Heaven* [P], where the artist has used the Byzantine iconography which represented the Ascension of Christ within a mandorla of light supported by Angels. Below is the empty sepulcher of *Mary,* with the *Apostles* in adoration.

Lastly comes *Christ and the Virgin Mary Enthroned* [Q]. This is considered one of the masterpieces of medieval painting in the West, in particular for the way in which the perspective of the great throne is rendered (an iconography at the time widespread in the East and in highly complex variants, even with circular thrones). The benediction of Christ, through the intercession of *Mary,* thus descends on the *Franciscan Friars* who, after the Chapter of Pisa in 1269, were particularly devoted to Her.

The three two-light windows in the apse are particularly important because they are among the few examples of medieval Italian stained glass that has come down to us. During the 12th and 13th centuries contacts between the French and imperial courts and the East had led to the introduction of imposing cycles of stained-glass windows in the large churches across the Alps. In Italy the technical skills had been lost and only Venice had received, through Byzantium, the great old legacy of the production of stained glass, but without ever achieving the wealth and splendor of the northern examples. While a few cathedrals in Italy did have stained-glass windows, extant examples are dramatically few.

The stained-glass windows in Assisi are therefore a practically unique chapter, in size and intrinsic value, in Italian art history. Those of the apse in particular constitute a real evangelical cycle with the *Stories of Christ: His Public Life*, the *Passion*, while the panels with the scenes of the *Childhood of Christ* were redone in the 1920s. Next to them, in the openings near the two-light windows, are the *Stories of the Old Testament*, reaffirming, like the ones on the walls, that "concordance between the Old and New Testaments" in the frescoes of the Nave.

Apparently the stained glass in the apse was among the first to be made by a German Master, close to the workshops in the Church of the Discalced Friars in Erfurt in Germany, and by a second artist, probably Austrian, with a vast knowledge of the Byzantine idiom. Both artists were, in any case, strongly influenced by the characteristic German style (so-called "*Zackenstil*"), with broken angular folds, with respect to the French Gothic, above all in its strong Byzantine inspiration. On the whole art historians believe this inspiration to have come via Venice, but the problem is complex and is dependent on the dating of the stained glass.

Most recent studies date them to 1255. Many scholars believe they were made shortly before the upper church was consecrated (1253) while others believe they were made much earlier, by 1239 when Brother Elias was still Minister of the Order. If this were so, it would be particularly interesting from a historical point of view, for it would mean that the allover project for the apse structure would have to date to that period, clearly anticipating the construction of the transept set against the nave (the stained-glass windows had to be made to precise measurements).

Whatever the case, if they do date to before 1253, in other words before the return of Pope Innocent IV to Italy after being forced to stay away by Frederick II, and if, above all, the windows were made

Apse, the papal throne and the choir stalls before the earthquake of 1997

in Erfurt, capital of Thuringia, the patronage of Emperor Frederick II returns to the fore, for he maintained close ties with Thuringia. The queen of the German State, Elisabeth of Hungary, a cousin of the emperor, had become a Franciscan Tertiary and was canonized in 1235 by Pope Gregory IX. The following year Frederick wrote to Brother Elias, in Assisi, to inform him of Elisabeth's solemn funeral in Marburg, where she was then buried. Artistic relations between Erfurt and Assisi could well have been mediated by Frederick II at whose court there were obviously numerous groups of German artisans. This would also explain the strong Byzantine influence apparent in these windows, coming not so much from Venice as from the relationship of the Emperor with the provincial Despotates of the East.

Inside an aedicule at the center of the apse is the *papal throne* [b], made by Roman marble workers around the middle of the 13th century. The aedicule consists of two columns of red marble which support an architrave with imitation mosaic decoration (as was the custom in the Roman circles and as can be seen in some of the scenes of the *Franciscan stories*), with a triangular pediment with a

Apse, view of the papal throne after the choir stalls were dismantled after the earthquake of 1997

trilobate aperture in the center. The throne is raised up on a base sculptured with ferocious royal and fantastic animals (a *lion*, an *asp*, a *dragon* and a *basilisk*) over which the papal power symbolically asserts itself.

ALTAR
The *high altar* [a] was consecrated in 1253 by Pope Innocent IV. Two secondary altars were then installed in the transept arms but were later removed. The high altar stands on a podium and consists of a slab of red Assisi marble with Cosmati panels at the sides.

Sanctuary, Cimabue, Vaults of the *Evangelists*

CROSSING VAULTS: the *Evangelists*

The four vault sections above the sanctuary act as a connecting link between the *Stories of the Life of the Virgin* in the apse and the *Via Sacra* in the nave in expressing the history of the Church. The vaults are frescoed with figures of the *Four Evangelists*, who wrote the four books of the Gospels, the only neo-testamentary Sacred Scriptures recognized by the Church as the story of the teachings of Christ (the so-called *Apocrypha* were never canonically accepted). The figures of the Evangelists are also associated, in the name of the diffusion of the word of Christ through the Church, with stylized depictions of cities, which refer to evangelized countries.

The vaults were painted, according to the art historians, by the Florentine painter Cimabue, who thus played a part in Assisi in a moving away from the Gothic Angevin style towards the rediscovery of classical antiquity that characterized the Roman circles where the artist had spent some time (1272). In line with the more modern

Sanctuary, Vaults of the *Evangelists* after the earthquake of 1997

trends of Byzantine painting, the *Evangelists* are no longer shown in their sacral poses, but as men devoted to their terrestrial task. The same attention to the depiction of real space is shown in the desks and chairs of the Evangelists as they transcribe the words of Christ.

On the north side we have the section with the figure of *Saint Mark* and of "*Ytalia*", with reference specifically to Rome and its monuments, as well as the coat of arms of the Orsini family on the Campidoglio where the city Senate had its headquarters. The period when the vault was made can be established thanks to this emblem, for the family obtained a senate title between 1278 and 1280, during the pontificate of Nicholas III Orsini (before and after that period the title was held by a member of the House of Anjou).

In 1279 the Orsini pope definitively integrated the Franciscans into the ecclesiastical institution, and the Church took over ownership of the monks' buildings.

In the view of Rome in *Ytalia*, the precisely described monuments include the Senate palace, the basilica of Saint Peter (with the large mosaic Pope Gregory IX had had made), the Pantheon (with part of the original inscription) and Castel Sant'Angelo (with Hadrian's frieze).

In the west section, adjacent to the apse, is *Saint Luke* with reference to Greece (indicated as "*Ipn-acchaia*" as was customary in the Middle Ages) and, in particular, Corinth, the most important city at the time.

On the south side is the section with the figure of *Saint John*, who spread Christianity in Asia (the reference here is to the city of *Ephesos*, now in Turkey).

The east vault adjacent to the nave with the figure of *Saint Matthew* and *Judea* (with Jerusalem) is one of those that fell in the undulatory earthquake of 1997 and demonstrated that the nave and the transept of the upper church are basically two independent bodies, even though joined together, and that they were built in two different phases (which might be very close chronologically, but differed in structural techniques). The way in which the Basilica reacted to the principal seismic movements was somewhat like that of the wagons of a train (the individual bays) shaken in an E-W direction, since in the Franciscan complex the buttresses (solid cylindrical towers with flying buttresses, capable of withstanding stress) are located only in a N-S direction. In the frequently deplored restorative consolidation of the 1950s reinforced concrete beams were inserted above the Basilica vaults, thus bonding together the bays and transforming the upper part of the building into a "battering ram" (an example of how restoration that changes the static balance of a historical building can be extremely harmful).

Nave and sanctuary,
The vaults reconstructed in their 'neutral' form after the earthquake of 1997

In a railroad collision, comparable to a strong undulatory shock, the locomotive and the last car are generally the ones to be derailed. In other words the external points where the horizontal thrusts transmitted by the cars in the middle would end up. In the Basilica, struck by various shocks in 1997 like blows of a battering ram in the E-W and W-E direction, the vault with *Saint Jerome* fell because it was the outermost one facing east and part of the Giottesque paintings on the barrel vault adjacent to the facade with *Saint Francis, Saint Clare* and other *saints*. The facade, without sustaining buttresses, acts here as a simple vault and therefore has no specific static function in containing the thrust. Things would have been different if, for example, there had been towers on the facade.

The vault with *Saint Matthew* to the west collapsed in a parallel direction. If the nave had been perfectly joined to the transept (and only the arms of the transept had been built later), the vault with *Saint Luke*, or even the apse itself, would probably have collapsed. What fell however was the vault with *Saint Matthew*, that is the first in the transept adjacent to the nave with must have had a N-S construction direction It is therefore highly likely that the last vault section in the nave transferred the thrust produced by the quake to the adjacent vault section, which then collapsed, because the transept has shown itself to be a sort of autonomous rigid body.

Human lives were lost and the art was also seriously damaged.

CHOIR STALLS

The wooden choir stalls [Co], which run along the entire western wall of the basilica, are a fine example of late 15th century cabinet work and were commissioned by Pope Sixtus IV in 1491, through

Apse, the fifteenth-century choir stalls

the Minister General Francesco Nani known as Sansone. The craftsmen, such as the cabinet maker Francesco Indovini, came from the Sienese and Urbino milieu close to Francesco di Giorgio Martini.

NORTH ARM OF THE TRANSEPT: the so-called "Maestro Oltramontano" and his assistants, Jacopo Torriti and Cimabue

Apparently it was Pope Clement IV (1265-1268), closely tied to the house of Anjou, who first commissioned the frescoes in the north arm of the transept. The Angevin emblem, the lily, appears frequently in the transept and it was under the pontificate of Clement IV that Charles I of Anjou obtained the throne of Naples by defeating Manfred, son of Frederick II, in 1266. The paintings in this arm of the transept are therefore those which most reveal the presence of French-Angevin painters in Assisi, as well as, perhaps, a few English masters.

The work of a talented painter in the French style, with assistants, has been identified in the upper zones. The circle and rosette decoration of the surfaces on either side of the large quadrifore, as well as the stained glass, is also extremely unified as in the cathedrals beyond the Alps. In the gallery (walkway) the backgrounds behind the Apostles are a compact red and blue, while the large robust heads of the figures with their strongly marked features, when compared with French examples of the time, indicate a date around 1270. The drapery is lively and broken up into folds of an expressionistic type close to contemporary painting in England. The two expressive stories with "animated linear effects" in the lunettes in the northwest and northeast walls can be related to Franco-English miniature painting. The figures of *David* and *Elijah* in the head of the transept (north wall) are more articulated, and the shape of the space in which the figures are contained echoes that of the window nearby, just as in a Gothic cathedral. The effect is enhanced by the steep triangular pediments of the painted gallery, clearly alluding to those of the French cathedrals. The most important works have therefore been tied in with the so-called "Maestro Oltremontano", who had also begun to paint the vault of the choir which was then finished by Cimabue.

On the end wall and, above all on the north-east wall, the northern painter was flanked by an artist whose style was quite different, probably related to the Roman milieu. He abolished the two-colored backgrounds and used forms of classic derivation in the decorations and drapery. He probably replaced the Maestro Oltremontano in a second phase of the work: for many he is to be identified with Jacopo Torriti.

THE NORTHWEST WALL to the right of the apse: the *Doctors of the Church* and *Saint Peter* by Cimabue and his assistants

The wall once more is divided into three registers. In the uppermost one is *God in Majesty Surrounded by the Symbols of the Evangelists* [R], who with their works – the Gospels – constituted the basic texts for the foundation of the norms of the Church.

After the figures of the *Angels* [An] on high and the *Apostles* [Ap] further down, in the middle register, to mediate between Heaven and earth, are scenes of the *Life of Saint Peter*, designated by Christ as founder of the Church ("you are Peter and on this stone I will found my Church"), with particular attention to the conversions his miracles worked, according to the *Acts of the Apostles* and the *Golden Legend* by Jacobus de Voragine, a popular medieval text.

Left, *Peter Healing a Lame Man* [S] by Cimabue. Peter, bending over the lame man, heals him by laying on his hands. When compared to many of the scenes attributed to the same artist, here the study of space is particularly attentive and close to his style in the later Franciscan stories in the nave.

North transept, northwest wall,
Cimabue, *Saint Peter Healing a Lame Man*

The closest references are once more those of 13th century Byzantine painting. The building at the center with its octagonal shape is probably a baptistery (although some have identified it as the Pantheon).

On the right, *Peter Heals the Sick and Liberates Those Possessed from Demons* [T] by Cimabue. Peter, at the center of the scene, raises his arm and miracles are accomplished by this gesture.

North transept, northwest wall, Cimabue, *Saint Peter Healing the Sick*

THE NORTH WALL: *Saint Peter and Saint Paul*

In the highest register on the north wall, on either side of the large quadrifore, are the *prophet Elijah* [El] on the left and *King David* [Da] on the right.

The S*tories of Saint Peter* continue in the register below to which the stories of *Saint Paul,* another eminent founder of the Church, are added. Francis was particularly devoted to both of these "Apostles of the people". As in the facing wall of the south transept and in each bay of the nave, the scenes are divided into three panels.

On the left, the *Fall of Simon Magus* [U], where the kneeling Saint Paul is shown as well as Saint Peter. The story is taken from an Apocrypha, the *Apocryphal Acts of Saint Peter,* but had been included in the *Golden Legend* and frescoed in the portico of the old Vat-

North transept, north wall,
Cimabue, the *Fall of Simon Magus*
Below: north transept, north wall,
Cimabue, the *Martyrdom of Saint Peter*

ican basilica. Once more note the great care Cimabue paid to depicting spatial depth, with the succession of planes and with increasingly studied points of view.

At the center is the *Martyrdom of Saint Peter* [V], where the scene is set between two monuments of antiquity still extant in Rome: the Pyramid of Caius Cestius, and the Meta Romulii, with which Cimabue was evidently personally acquainted.

On the right the *Martyrdom of Saint Paul* [Z] (fragmentary) is shown.

The great quadrifore is richly decorated with stained glass narrating the *Stories of Christ* in the moments after his death, from his first apparition to the *Ascension*. In this case the date must be later than the quadrifore on the south wall and seems to be the work of the Umbrian workshop of the Figline Master, active in many other stained-glass windows in the Franciscan complex.

Left: **North transept, view of the four-light opening**
Right: **north transept, detail of the four-light opening**

THE NORTHEAST WALL: the *primitive Church*

The Story of the primitive Church, which originated at the foot of the Cross and then at the moment of the *Descent of the Holy Spirit*, is summed up, in a convincing parallelism with the symmetrical wall of the south transept.

The lowermost register is taken up by the *Crucifixion* [A*], with *Longinus*, who was then converted and became a Saint, as a symbol of the redemption of the pagans. On the right is *Saint Francis* embracing the Cross, to indicate his perfect identification with Christ and his full faithfulness to the teachings of the Master. On the left is the *Virgin Mary* together with the *pious women* (an evident identification with the Franciscan Poor Clares) and, then, a group of *Pharisees*, the learned Jews who opposed the teachings of Christ (a clear allusion to the difficulties Francis encountered in the Roman ecclesiastical world). In this scene Cimabue has given us the moment of the verification of the death of *Christ*, with *Longinus* who touches his ribs with his lance and *Mary* fainting. This contrasts with the corresponding scene on the south transept where *Christ* was still alive and entrusted his *mother Mary* to *John*.

In the middle register, in the gallery, are the *twelve Apostles* [Ap], in the place of the *angels* in the corresponding position on the wall of the south transept; and above, the *Angels* [An].

In the uppermost part, in the lunette (third register), the *Transfigu-*

ration of Christ [B*] is shown, corresponding to the *Christ in Glory* on the wall of the south transept. But in this image of Christ in a mandorla of light, it is the figures next to him in the Heavens who are stressed: *Moses* (who had received the Commandments), *Elijah* (the prophet of salvation), and, at his feet, *Saint Peter* (founder of the Church), *Saint James* and *Saint John* (to whom Christ had entrusted Mary).

North transept, view of the northeast wall

North transept, northeast wall, Cimabue, the *Crucifixion*

THE NAVE
Saint Francis and the concordance between the Old and New Testaments

The fame of the nave – the fulcrum of the visit to the Franciscan complex – depends on the pictorial cycle of the *Life of Saint Francis*. These rather complex scenes were originally meant to be a continuing education for the brothers to remind them, through images, of a series of Truths and Principles (from the Old Testament to Salvation) in which the role assigned to Francis was inevitable. It was in other words a great 'encyclopedia' of Faith with numerous levels of interpretation which depended on the theological background of the individual. The correct term nowadays would be "inter-textual", a search for increasingly complex and refined meanings, using mnemonic techniques involving the remembering of images. The intentions of the pictures were not however purely abstract, for the mendicant friars used these landscapes, relations, recollections in their sermons. This tale, based on Saint Bonaventure of Bagnoregio's *Legenda maior* of 1266, was

View of the Nave and the sanctuary after the restoration undertaken after the earthquake of 1997. *On pages 168-169:* The nave looking towards the inner facade after the restorations which followed the earthquake of 1997

not only an educational 'exercise' for the Brothers, but also the 'correct' interpretation, as seen by the Order, which Franciscans all over the world were to furnish of the episodes in the Life of Francis (in particular the more 'problematical' ones), and his identification with Christ (*Franciscus alter Christus*). Bonaventure himself said that his story of the *Life* was not in any specific chronological order, but followed a criteria of the 'importance' of the events in transmitting a coherent story. The same happens on the walls of the nave which shows the official less subversive version, especially after the bitter struggles between the Franciscan Conventuals and the Franciscan Spirituals. In 1260 the Chapter of the Order, preoccupied by the diffusion of various versions of the *Life of Francis* which pictured him as a saint free from ecclesiastic schemes and embittered by the betrayal of his radical concept of evangelical poverty, ordered all unauthorized *Lives* to be burned, for they did nothing but create confusion within the church itself, and entrusted Bonaventure with writing a new version. The result was a Francis who was so perfect that any attempt to imitate him in his ideals of total poverty would not only have been pointless, but outright dangerous.

This was not however enough to placate the souls and in 1323 Pope John XXII declared that the idea of the poverty of Christ and his Apostles (which Francis had taken as model) was heretical, and once more persecuted the Spirituals. The moderation of the frescoes in the nave of Assisi is thus an example of sanctity within the limits of orthodoxy, stressing the fact that the Franciscan complex was of fundamental importance for all of Catholicism, in the conformity of the life of Francis to the story of Salvation and the Church, as well as to the life of Christ as told in the *Gospels*.

A single iconographic program therefore governed the realization of the frescoes in the upper church from the transept to the nave, except for a few modifications in the course of execution. This is also why the artistic style had to be basically unified, without gross discontinuities between the various phases which stretched over a period of almost thirty years and which can be thought of as 'lots' of a single workshop. This is why different scenes contain the same gestures, the same decoration, the same iconographic subjects, even the silhouettes of the same personages. It can also be noted how many masters (such as the one known as "della Cattura" or of the Capture of Christ or the Master of the "Way to Calvary", after the scenes attributed to them) who were already present in the Cimabue phase, continued to work afterwards and sought to adapt their style to the newer style of the Master of the Franciscan Stories

(Giotto or Cavallini). These scenes were therefore not all on the same artistic level, although they were all in line with a basic program which has led art historians to speak of Giotto's large and highly organized "Workshop" (if the best subjects are attributed to his hand).

But while, as in Bonaventure, the scenes in the nave do not respect a precise chronological order of the events in the life of Francis, neither were the Franciscan panels painted beginning at one end of the wall and moving on to the other. In an attempt to understand what really happened, close range analyses have been done in the last fifty years to identify the plaster strata. In the scenes in the nave, for instance, the fresco technique was that of the '*giornata*' or 'day patch' which consisted of applying only the amount of intonaco that could be painted in a single day.

The scaffolding was moved as needed, for the humidity on the walls might vary or the underlying masonry might not always be perfectly homogeneous. Generally the uppermost parts were done before the lower parts, so the colors would not run downwards. If a single day's intonaco had not yet dried, then another patch some distance away might be started, so as not to interrupt the work. It is not easy to identify these strata for the artists always tried to mask the breaks between one day's work and the next. The scene with *Francis Honored by a Simple Man* (scene I) was one of the last to be painted, and the panel with *Francis Giving Away his Cloak* (scene II) was done after the *Dream of the Palace Filled with Weapons* (scene III). They were all done in phases and the first to have been completely finished was that of *Francis Before the Crucifix at San Damiano* (scene IV).

The complexity of the Franciscan cycle required a basic allover design, which was put on the first layer of plaster (uncolored scratch coat) in a sketch in red earth, the so-called sinopia. A small fragment of the sinopia is visible above the halo of Francis in the scene (XVII) of the *Sermon in the Presence of Honorius III* where the intonaco has fallen off. In general it is to be noted that the buildings in the background of the panels on the south wall (on the left for those who enter from the main entrance) are more complex than those on the right hand wall. Space is much more carefully represented and although a correct one-point perspective has not been achieved (it was not worked out organically until the 15th century, with Humanism), everything seems to be subordinated to precise geometric lines, and all those drawn freehand disappear. Together with the variations in the poses of the figures identified by Bruno Zanardi and the use of different techniques for the skin coloring, this aspect has led to the identification of pauses in the work, perhaps even a replacement of workmen and entire artist workshops. Aside from the difficult artistic problems regarding the frescoes, physically and iconographically the upper church is consistently organized. The nave has been divided into four bays with cross vaults. Each wall of each bay has been articulated into three super-posed registers, with the uppermost and the middle register in turn divided in two by the presence of the large windows. The lowermost register is subdivided into three scenes per bay within a single architectural frame (as if we were face to face with a portico with three apertures) and a continuous narration.

It is therefore necessary to stand at the center of each bay, below the keystone in the vault, for a complete interpretation which can be done by:

a) Reading in a horizontal sense along the walls.
This is unquestionably the most immediate interpretation of the succession of scenes.
- On the north wall (on the right for those who enter, but originally on the left) are the *Stories of the Old Testament*, beginning in the zone closest to the transept, above in the two registers. In the lowest register are the *Stories of Saint Francis* (beginning with the fourth bay near the transept).
– On the south wall (left for those who enter, but originally on the right) the *Stories of Christ* begin on the area closest to the transept, and in the lowest register, in an unbroken band, the *Stories of Saint Francis* continue, unifying the story.
– The vault sections of the nave contain the images of the founders and organizers of the Church: the inner facade is connected to this program with, above, images referring to the Church, while below are two added scenes regarding the *Stories of Saint Francis*.

b) Reading in a vertical sense for each wall of each bay.
Various levels of theological interpretation come to the fore in this type of reading. They aim to relate the episodes from the *Life of Francis* with various events in the *Old Testament* (on the right) and in the *New Testament* (on the left). There are 'more immediate' comparisons and others which only a careful in-depth interpretation can discover. The general idea however is that of identifying Francis with Adam, Abraham, Isaac, Joseph and, lastly, in the scenes that cover the whole left wall, with Christ.

c) Reading per bay, relating the scenes on opposing walls (right and left) of each bay.
This was probably the level in which allegorical interpretation

achieved its zenith in the reading of the cycle, with a profound conceptual rigor governing the relationship between one scene and the next. This is the most difficult level of comprehension of which only a general outline can be furnished here.

NORTH (or RIGHT) WALL OF THE NAVE: the continuity between the History of the People of Israel and the Franciscan message

FOURTH BAY
a) Horizontal reading of the Franciscan register: the *Life of Saint Francis*

Nave, north wall, fourth bay, the frescoes of the register of the *Franciscan stories*

Scene I) *Saint Francis Honored by a Simple Man*
The episode, which is first mentioned in the *Legenda maior* by Saint Bonaventure (I,1), is inspired by a paragraph in the Gospels regarding the entry of Christ into Jerusalem, when cloaks were laid down on the ground before him as in this depiction in Assisi. Bonaventure's *Life of Saint Francis* moreover aimed at stressing this identity between Christ and Francis. Just as the Lord began his Calvary, so Francis in this entry began his way towards La Verna, where he then received the stigmata. The halo around his head shows that he is already on the way to sainthood. The depiction of the *Piazza Comunale* of Assisi in the background is particularly interesting. At the center is the Roman temple, previously transformed into a church (note the rose window in the gable) and then a prison (identified by the grates in the windows). This is however a symbolic rather than real image for this temple has five columns and not six (with a column on the central axis, where the entrance should be) and in the gable there are angels supporting the rose window, indicating the Christianization of the building. The tower on the left

Nave, north wall, fourth bay, Giotto (or Pietro Cavallini) and assistants, *Saint Francis Honored by a Simple Man* (sc. I)

would also seem to refer to reality, for the top part has not yet been terminated. This was done in 1305, which has led to dating the entire cycle as prior to this date, since this scene was one of the last to be painted in line with the succession of applications of intonaco. Some historians however believe that the panel was painted to replace an earlier one, which raises problems regarding the stratification of the plaster layers as well as the theological interpretation of the cycle. Others believe that it was particularly difficult to paint this scene because of the beams of the iconostasis, the partition separating the nave from the space of the monks. Confirmation of the fact that it was executed at the end of the long artistic itinerary of the entire cycle of the *Life of Saint Francis* can be deduced from the treatment of the garments and flesh tones, much more delicate when compared with the harsher colors and strokes in the scene nearby where *Francis Gives Away his Cloak*.

Scene II) *Francis Gives his Cloak to a Poor Man*
Francis is indicated as a new Christ and also as a new Saint Martin,

172

Nave, north wall, fourth bay, Giotto (or Pietro Cavallini) and assistants, *Saint Francis Gives his Cloak to a Poor Man* (sc. II)

in his renunciation of earthly riches.

In commemorating this act of Francis, the iconographic program which governed the whole cycle stressed his adherence to the evangelical precept "clothe the naked", as well as comparing the figure of the new Saint with that of the Good Samaritan and, above all, of Saint Martin. The lines of the surrounding landscape (the City of Assisi is on the left on Monte Asio and the Monastery of Saint Benedict on Subasio is on the right) converge in the halo around Francis' head, geometrically set at the center of the scene. It has been noted that this scene is a symbolic example of how events considered subversive were modified: according to Francis' Testament, dictated shortly before he died, he had met some lepers and this had made him change his life, moving him to compassion. In Bonaventure's *Legenda maior* (I,2), the lepers are replaced by a "poor and ill-dressed knight" because evidently the contact of Francis with the lepers was still too raw for his contemporaries. The knight moreover is shown as a decorous citizen, even if rather down at the heels. The

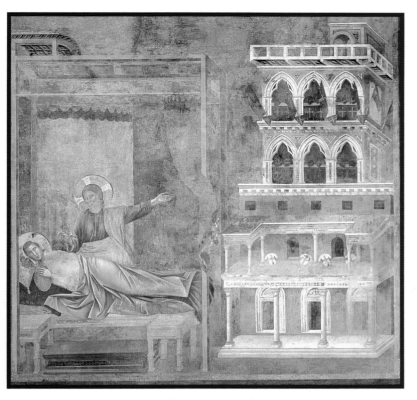

Nave, north wall, fourth bay, Giotto (or Pietro Cavallini) and assistants, the *Vision of the Palace Full of Weapons* (sc. III)

extreme poverty the Franciscans professed was one of the major reasons for their contrasts with the ecclesiastical hierarchies and authorities in the city, and on several occasions popes and cardinals attempted to mitigate it. From a point of view of style, close affinities, in the sharp planes, undercuts and harsh colors, have been noted between this scene, the scenes painted first in this cycle and the *Stories of Isaac*. This is confirmed by the attempts at creating chiaroscuro, close to Cimabue's technique, and of hatching in the color. The city gate in the city walls, in the foreground, is probably that of Santa Chiara, creating an element of precise realistic allusion (even if not completely accurate).

Scene III) *The Dream of the Palace Filled with Weapons in Spoleto*
Francis renounces his youthful desires and the greatest terrestrial glories.
The *Legend of the Three Companions* and in part the *First* and *Second Life* by Thomas of Celano, tell the story of how Francis, before

his conversion, was a young man who took part in wars, and that in 1205 he had offered to fight in the war in Puglia, as well as participating in the unfortunate undertakings of Assisi against Perugia. He was taken prisoner by the Perugines and after returning to Assisi, Francis started out for Puglia. In Spoleto he was taken with a high fever and had a vision of Christ who invited him to renounce military glory and his aspiration to knighthood, just as Christ had appeared in a dream to Saint Martin after he had given half of his cloak to a poor man. Thus in the lower part of the building which represents Francis' house in Assisi, his weapons can be seen abandoned forever, heaped up in disorder. Up above are the standards, carefully put away and never again to be taken up, according to Bonaventure's tale (I,3). The image of the house is truly interesting. It is shown as a rich merchant's palace, a building closed at the bottom (the warehouse) and with large windows on the upper floors (the actual residence). A rich loggia is set before the entrance, with its three richly decorated doors. It has been suggested that two different palaces are shown here but it seems more likely that it is a single dwelling.

These first three scenes close with a dream in which Francis is the protagonist. The second trio, in the following bay, will also close with a dream – symmetrically – although of the Pope.

b) Vertical reading of the wall: the *Old Testament* and *Saint Francis* First register above divided by the window: on the left the *Creation of the World* [1] (or the *Separation of Light from Dark* by Jacopo Torriti) and, on the right, the *Creation of Adam* [2] by Jacopo Torriti.

Middle register divided by the window: Left: *Noah Building the Ark* [9] (by Jacopo Torriti) and, on the right, *Noah Entering the Ark* [10] (or the *Flood* by Jacopo Torriti).

According to the art historian Supino, the drawing of the features, the hair and beards, the placement of the heads in these *Stories of Noah* repeat elements in the frescoes in the apse of Santa Maria Maggiore in Ro-

Nave, north wall, fourth bay, Jacopo Torriti, the *Creation of the World*

Nave, fourth bay, view of the north wall

me, strongly indicating that they were painted by a Roman painter such as Torriti.

From the theological point of view, the scenes in this bay are all centered on a message referring to the transience of earthly things, which however are always God-given. God created the world and man, but then God can also decide to destroy Creation, with the Flood, saving only those who believe in Him (Noah). Thus the abandonment of earthly possessions by Francis, which he had received from God, can be compared to the loss of the world before the Flood and then to the salvation of Noah.

c) Reading of the two walls (right and left) of the bay
Layout of the scenes:

NORTH WALL	SOUTH WALL
FIRST REGISTER ABOVE	
Creation of the World [1]	*Annunciation* [1*]
Creation of Adam [2]	*Visitation* [2*]
MIDDLE REGISTER	
Building the Ark [9]	*Wedding in Cana* [9*]
Noah Entering the Ark [10]	*Raising of Lazarus* [10*]
FRANCISCAN REGISTER	
sc. I) *Saint Francis Honored*	sc. XXVIII) *Liberation of the Penitent Heretic*
sc. II) *Gift of the Cloak*	sc. XXVII) *Confession of a Woman Restored to Life*
sc. III) *Dream of the Palace*	sc. XXVI) *Healing of a Devoted Follower*

Left: **Nave, fourth bay, view of the north wall**
Right: **Nave, fourth bay view of the south wall**

THIRD BAY

a) Horizontal reading of the Franciscan register: the *Life of Saint Francis*

Nave, north wall, third bay, frescoes of the register of the *Franciscan stories*

Scene IV) *Saint Francis in Prayer before the Crucifix of San Damiano*
Francis is called directly by God.

As narrated in the *Legenda maior* of Saint Bonaventure (II,1), while Francis was praying before the wooden *Crucifix* at the time in San Damiano (now in the Chapel of San Giorgio in Santa Chiara) Christ spoke to the future saint three times, inviting him to "repair the house of Christ". The *Crucifix* was located in a small church in ruins. Francis thought that the invitation of Christ referred to San Damiano, but the Lord had other plans for him, delegating him a task that involved the entire Church. To be noted is the *Crucifix* painted in a pre-12th century Byzantine style, with the Christ alive on the Cross (*Christus triumphans*) and not suffering (*Christus patiens*). The left part of the small Church was later repainted in the course of restoration to eliminate an unpleasant visual effect due to the detachment of the original plaster. The building appears here as it was before Francis began to restore it, traditionally replacing the original timber roof with vaulting. For later Franciscan building this was of great importance. Francis had said that the churches should be decorous, but not excessively rich. The principle of poverty followed by the Spirituals of the Order initially decreed that all the Franciscan churches should be simple naves with a timber covering, often resting on masonry arches. Where possible, the Conventuals covered their churches with vaults, as in the complex of Assisi, basing themselves on what Francis had done in San Damiano and in the name of a structural solidity which would eliminate the inherent weaknesses of wood.

Scene V) *The Renouncement of Worldly Goods: Saint Francis makes*

Nave, north wall, third bay, Giotto (or Pietro Cavallini) and assistants, *Saint Francis Praying before the Crucifix in San Damiano* (sc. IV)

the decision, dictated by faith, to renounce his inheritance and earthly possessions

The attitude taken by Francis is not that of a heretic who wishes to set himself outside the Church, and he is benevolently received by the bishop of Assisi, whose role is therefore fundamental. In this scene, which takes place in the square in front of the Bishop's Palace, the tale told in Bonaventure's *Legenda maior* (II,4) is enriched by details taken from the *Tale of the Three Companions*. Francis, repudiated by his father, who like his fellow citizens believe him to be mad, takes off all his clothes, which were part of the family patrimony. On the left (the part of the iniquitous) is his father, who attempts to fling himself on his son, but is held back by his wrist by a notable citizen. As told in the story of the *Three Companions*, some children (here once more on the left) then chased Francis from the city, throwing stones at him as was usual with the mentally deranged. On the right (the part of the just), the Bishop

Nave, north wall, third bay, Giotto (or Pietro Cavallini) and assistants, *Saint Francis Renouncing His Worldly Goods* (sc. V)

of Assisi covers the naked Francis (unacceptable in church) while, in heaven above, the hand of God the Father blesses him. For the first time Francis is set on the right of the scene: his conversion has finally taken place.

Scene VI) *The Dream of Pope Innocent III, in which he recognizes the mission of Francis, who is supporting the Lateran Basilica*
The indispensability of the work of Francis in the design of God. Pope Innocent III has a dream in which the Lateran basilica – the whole Church – is collapsing and a single figure – Francis – saves it. Francis has already taken Poverty as his bride and wears the habit, which will now identify him and differs from the cloaks in the preceding scenes. With his work, he becomes the 'load-bearing column' of the Church. To be noted is how the decorative aspects and the various "hands" appear highly unified (aside from the fact that those *Stories* too have been attributed to the young Giotto). The

Nave, north wall, third bay, Giotto (or Pietro Cavallini) and assistants, the *Dream of Pope Innocent III* (sc. VI)

Lateran basilica also looks very realistic, and even has the mosaic tondos made around the 1290s under Pope Nicholas IV.

b) Vertical reading of the wall: The *Old Testament* and *Saint Francis*
First register above divided by the window: on the left *Creation of Eve* [3] (Jacopo Torriti) and, on the right, the *Original Sin* [4] (Jacopo Torriti).
Middle register divided by the window: on the left the *Sacrifice of Abraham* [11] (Jacopo Torriti or the young Giotto) and, on the right the *Visit of the Angels to Abraham* [12] (the obvious repainting of this scene makes any hypothesis as to the original artist impossible).
According to the art historian Supino, the scene of the *Sacrifice of Abraham* is stylistically close to the *Stories of Noah* in the fourth bay, and should be connected to the work of Jacopo Torriti. Today art historians however tend to attribute these scenes to the young Giotto, an example of how difficult it is to know who painted what, and

Nave, third bay, view of the north wall

how the most authoritative opinions are modified in time. Only the angels remain from the *Visit of the Angels,* and they have been so repainted that no hypotheses as to the artist can be broached.

Read in relation to the scenes in the upper registers, the episodes from the life of Saint Francis shown in this bay depict him as the new Abraham, a comparison made by Bonaventure in a few passages in his story (III,10). The central theme of this comparison is that family values are always subordinate to the desires of God. Both Abraham and Francis had in fact abandoned everything, and had above all renounced family love to follow the orders of the Lord.

c) Reading of the two walls (right and left) of the bay
Scheme of the scenes:

NORTH WALL	SOUTH WALL
FIRST REGISTER	
Creation of Eve [3]	*Nativity* [3*]
Original Sin [4]	*Adoration of the Magi* [4*]
MIDDLE REGISTER	
Sacrifice of Abraham [11]	*Capture of Christ* [11*]
Visit of the Angels	
to Abraham [12]	*Christ before Pilate* [12*]
FRANCISCAN REGISTER	
sc. IV) *Prayer in San Damiano*	sc. XXV) *The Apparition to Gregory IX*
sc. V) *Renouncement of Worldly Goods*	sc. XXIV) *Canonization of Saint Francis*
sc. VI) *Dream of Innocent III*	sc. XXIII) *The Mourning of the Poor Clares*

Left: **Nave, third bay, view of the north wall**
Right: **Nave, third bay, view of the south wall**

Nave, third bay, vaults, roundels

VAULTS OVER THE THIRD BAY: the origins of the primitive Church and of the new Church

In the west vault, towards the sanctuary, *Christ the Redeemer (Deesis)* is shown. On the south is the *Virgin Mary*. The image of *Saint Francis* appears in the east vault, in the direction of the main entrance. Towards the north is *Saint John the Baptist.*

SECOND BAY
a) Horizontal reading of the Franciscan register: the *Life of Saint Francis*

Nave, north wall, second bay,
The frescoes in the register of the *Franciscan stories*

Nave, north wall, second bay, Giotto (or Pietro Cavallini) and assistants,
Pope Innocent III Approves the Rule (sc. VII)

Scene VII) *Pope Innocent III Orally Approves the Franciscan Rule and
Gives his Blessing*
The scene refers to the complete orthodoxy of the Franciscan *Rule*,
despite the innovative impact it had on the life of the Church at the
time.
In the History of the Church this scene is an extremely important
moment for it implicitly counterposes the work of Francis to that
of the heretical currents, which had been put out of the Church,
and which so often in the course of the Middle Ages had launched
themselves against the papal power. The teachings of Francis,
especially with his vocation of absolute poverty, were highly sub-

versive with regards to current ecclesiastical trends, as were those of analogous movements such as the Albigensians in Provence, a movement which had been wiped out in a bath of blood only a few years earlier (1198). In the early 13th century a group of followers gathered around Francis, but he never openly criticized the conduct of the Papacy (although he did do so with reference to the individual local clergy). Francis had requested the approval of his new *Rule* of life from Pope Innocent III. Initially the welcome given Francis upon his arrival in Rome was rather hostile, even in Bonaventure's narration (III,10). This was the pope who had launched the crusade against the Albigensians, and he was fearful of a new heresy. This time however he could not refuse to approve the *Rule*, because it was composed of passages taken from the Gospels. But it remained an oral approval. An attempt has been made in this scene to highlight the fact that the followers of Francis had submitted to a real monastic order (as seen by the tonsure) but also that Francis had remained a lay figure (and is therefore untonsured). This scene has often been reworked and repainted because of its deep theological and political impact. The Pope returns a written *Rule* to *Francis*, who kneels and is therefore submissive (originally he had been shown standing). Although this never really happened, it was something the Franciscan Order needed in the next few decades to stress its monastic and ecclesiastic status. There are eleven followers plus Francis in the scene on their way to Rome (Francis is the twelfth, perhaps to make sure there was no Judas). The *Rule* approved by Innocent III has been lost, or for some reason was not transmitted. The *Rule* of 1221 aroused such protests on the part of the Curia that it did not obtain papal approval. The final *Rule*, that of 1223, required considerable mediation and a great deal of censure before Pope Honorius III would grant approval. The scene is set in a large hall, the walls covered with great tapestries and hangings, as was customary in medieval times, and with arcading above, supported by decorated brackets.

Scene VIII) *The Vision of the Chariot of Fire: at Rivotorto the friars see Francis on a chariot of fire, like the early prophet Elijah*
The lay condition of Francis is assimilated to that of a prophet, since he had never taken the vows.
In the decades following his death the problem of the lack of an ecclesiastic status for Francis, who never took his vows, was a real problem for the Franciscan Order, which was vying with the Dominicans and hoped to be integrated into the religious hierarchies. To justify this 'difficult' status of the Founder, in his *Legenda*

Nave, north wall, second bay, Giotto (or Pietro Cavallini) and assistants, the *Vision of the Chariot of Fire* (sc. VIII)

maior (IV,4) Bonaventure evoked the fact that a chariot of fire, splendid as the sun, had appeared to the first Franciscans in Rivotorto, establishing a sort of analogy between Francis, who at the time lived in a hovel near the cathedral of San Rufino, and the prophet Elijah who was defined as the "guide of the true Israelites" in the Old Testament. To make this point even clearer, the scene goes beyond Bonaventure's tale and places Francis on the chariot, stressing his identification with Elijah who, as a prophet, was not a religious. The setting was also modified at the end of the 13th century on the basis of the new requirements of the Order: the *Legenda* narrates that the apparition took place in a hovel in the countryside of Rivotorto, while here the hut is replaced by a fine urban

Nave, north wall, second bay, Giotto (or Pietro Cavallini) and assistants, the *Vision of the Thrones in Paradise* (sc. IX)

building faced with marble. That vocation for absolute Poverty which had led the first Franciscans to live in secluded humble places was therefore banished from the official iconography. The chariot moreover recalls a Roman chariot, while the color of the horse refers to the biblical vision which mentions the tawny red horse as a symbol of health, of strength.

Scene IX) *The Vision of the Thrones in Paradise: Brother Pacifico has the vision of the throne in Paradise ready for Francis*
The glorification in the celestial orders of Francis and his followers to the highest ranks, to occupy the thrones in the place of other religious (the Dominicans?).

In this scene the glorification of the entire Order, and not only of Francis, begun in the preceding scene continues, in line with the story of Bonaventure (VI,6). Once more it is a humble friar who has the vision of the *heavenly thrones*, left empty by the Angels who fell to Hell and occupied by the *praying Francis* and his followers as indicated by the *Angel*. It should be noted that Francis is once more shown inside a finely decorated church, far from the ruins of the first San Damiano. The beauty of the world enters Franciscan life through the richly decorated altar cloth, and the walls and the base of the Crucifix, symbols of the costly commissions of an Order which is no longer a mendicant order and has been authorized to own property.

b) Vertical reading of the wall: the *Old Testament* and *Saint Francis*
First register above divided by the window: on the left *Expulsion from the Garden of Eden* [5] (Jacopo Torriti?) and, on the right, the *Labors of Adam and Eve* [6] (destroyed).
Middle register divided by the window: on the left *Isaac Blessing Jacob* [13] (or *Jacob's Deception* by the Isaac Master or the young Giotto) and, on the right *Esau before Isaac* [14] (by the Isaac Master or the young Giotto).
For some time now art historians have attributed these two scenes in their entirety to Giotto. The pictorial quality is outstanding, and at that date (c 1290) Giotto did not yet have a large workshop, as in later decades. These then would be his first works in the Franciscan basilica, apparent also in the sculptural treatment and occasional hard renderings of the figure, close to Cimabue, Giotto's teacher. Doubts however still remain as to whether they are by Giotto or not.
Whatever the case, the *Stories of Isaac* reveal a figurative innovation which goes beyond Cimabue's idiom, as well as the inauguration of a new technique in the use of fresco painting, replacing a vast stretch of plaster that went along the whole length of the scaffolding, to a "*giornata*" or day patch, of the amount of intonaco which could be painted in a single day. But more than anything it is the rendering of space, the realism of the setting that is apparent in the work of the Isaac Master, with the two scenes set in realist architectural settings in two volumes spatially articulated by the use of perspective. There are of course still 'shorthand' simplifications (as in the gables of the building above in the background) but these are 'tricks' encompassed in an overall desire to depict visible reality. When compared with what was being done some decades earlier, the transformation of the western pictorial scene and of the aesthetic canons does seem radical. Interest is no longer in convention, the model, an abstract perfection which had set real events in a spiritual sphere. The figures now acquire

Nave, second bay, view of the north wall

a naturalism which is far removed from the poses and stereotyped features (faces all alike, gestures all alike, garments all alike) formerly used
in the Byzantine art of the Comnene period (XII century). Contem-

Nave, second bay, middle register, Isaac Master (the young Giotto), *Isaac Blessing Jacob*

porary philosoph
was also beginning
to deal with the im
portance of experi
mentation and mat
ter even by the Fran
ciscan Friars. The
Stories of Isaac then
are an indication o
a profound renewa
of society that in
volved culture in
general and was no
limited to art. The
Master must cer
tainly have been
young, trained in
the new provincia
Byzantine currents
and no longer held
back – a question
of generation gap –
by the great masters
such as Cimabue
innovative as they
might have been

He was able to develop those principles of realism to the point where they could subvert an iconographic and figurative canon that had held for centuries.

In the scene of *Isaac Blessing Jacob*, the blind and dying Isaac raises himself from his bed, supported by a maid. He touches Jacob's right hand, covered with lambskin, and believes it to be the hand of his firstborn Esau who was particularly hairy (in the Near East hair was a symbol of impurity, so that, in the Bible, the condemnation of Esau was already implicit). Jacob appears accompanied by his mother Rebecca who had aided him in deceiving his old father and Esau. To be noted is the attempt to render space and the way in which the halo of Isaac, covers half of the maid's face, signifying what is 'in front' and what is 'behind'.

In his artistic maturity, if it is really Giotto (but it is doubtful), the artist was to abandon these symbolic spatial expedients (known as paratactic) to render space with a geometric structuring. The fresco is badly damaged, but Isaac's tired suffering face can still be seen.

The scene with *Esau before Isaac* is closely bound to the preceding scene and shows Esau who, after Jacob's deception, tries in vain to be recognized and obtain his father Isaac's blessing. *Jacob and Rebecca* flee on the right, while Esau is accompanied by his wife who, moreover, was not of the tribe of Israel but was a Cananite. Various perspective features here too are paratactic and not geometric in nature. Examples are the fingers of *Isaac's* hands which seem to diminish in depth, or in *Esau's* right hand holding

Nave, second bay, middle register, Isaac Master (young Giotto), *Esau before Isaac*

the spoon. The setting repeats that of the preceding scene, with Isaac's bed and the full drapes, previously held open by a servant and now shown closed. Curtains around the bed of a dead man was an iconography widespread in the 13th century and also appears in the sculptured tombs in the lower church in Assisi.

In this bay the accent is placed on the problem of the benedictions which were given by fathers or by the pope (the father of the Church) instead of directly by the Lord. Thus Francis is blessed by the pope, instituting a parallel with the story of Jacob. Brother Elias had called Francis the "second Jacob". The scene, however, seems to anticipate the problem of the blessing given by Francis upon his deathbed, as shown in scene XX. It is not known precisely on whom Francis had bestowed his blessing. To Brother Elias, of the Conventual branch of the Order, or to Bernardo, closer to the Franciscanism of the origins? Jacob's 'deception for the good' may here allude to the uncertain blessing probably misappropriated by Brother Elias, although after his excommunication Elias (1239) had been repudiated by the entire Franciscan hierarchy.

c) Reading of the two walls (right and left) of the bay
Scheme of the scenes:

NORTH WALL	SOUTH WALL
FIRST REGISTER	
Expulsion from the Garden of Eden [5]	*Presentation in the Temple*[5*]
Labors of Adam and Eve [6]	*Flight to Egypt* [6*]

MIDDLE REGISTER
Isaac Blessing Jacob [13]   *Way to Calvary* [13*]
Esau before Isaac [14]   *Crucifixion* [14*]

FRANCISCAN REGISTER
sc. VII) *Confirmation*   sc. XXII) *Confirmation of*
of the Rule   *the Stigmata*
sc. VIII) *Vision of the*   sc. XXI) *Vision of Fra Agostino*
Fiery Chariot
sc.IX) *Vision of the Heavenly*   sc. XX) *Death of Saint Francis*
Thrones

Left: **Nave, second bay, view of the north wall**
Right: **Nave, second bay, view of the south wall**

FIRST BAY

a) Horizontal reading of the Franciscan register: the *Public life of Saint Francis*

Nave, north wall, first bay, the frescoes of the register of the *Franciscan stories*

Scene X) *The Devils are cast out of Arezzo: Francis establishes peace in the city by driving the demons from Arezzo and that is defeating the Ghibellines*

The scene stresses the religious and political primacy of the Church with respect to the Empire.

In this scene too total attention is given to the concept of respect for the ecclesiastical hierarchies and the mandate of the Church, reaffirming the fact that the Franciscan Order, and Francis himself, had always remained within orthodoxy. The city of Arezzo, where *Francis* and one of his followers, *Brother Silvestro*, were staying, was devastated by demons: this was probably an allusion to the civil wars between Guelphs and Ghibellines which were raging in the medieval cities. The scene takes place in a city set up high on a hill protected by powerful walls. The devils, who seem to stand for the Ghibelline followers of Frederick II, are driven out by Silvestro, a consecrated priest (and therefore authorized for exorcism). Francis was a lay person and even though a saint, he could not assume the prerogatives of a priest and could only pray. Indeed, according to Bonaventure (VI,9), Francis asked Silvestro to exorcise the devils from the city. The message here is directed against all those heretical movements which were attempting to take over the prerogatives of the church. According to Chiara Frugoni, the enormous church behind *Francis* and *Silvestro* symbolizes the institution of the church, reaffirming the orthodoxy and correctness of the position taken by Francis and his followers. Elio Lunghi believes the building to be a more realistic representation of the Old Cathedral of Arezzo, which stood outside the city and was torn down by Cosimo I de'Medici in 1561.

Nave, north wall, first bay Giotto (or Pietro Cavallini) and assistants, the *Devils are Cast out from Arezzo* (sc. X)

In this scene we have a combination of a precise political message (the struggle against the Ghibelline faction) and a religious message (the struggle against heresy and the complete faithfulness to the Church of the Franciscan Order).

Scene XI) *Trial by Fire Before the Sultan: Francis successfully survives the ordeal by fire before the sultan of Egypt, a sign of the superiority of Christianity*
The scene reaffirms the primacy of the Christian faith over that of the infidels.
This scene is closely connected to the intentions expressed by Francis before Cardinal Ugolino (later Pope Gregory IX) of working for the salvation "of the entire world... in the lands of the infidels as well as in those of the Christians". Setting sail in Ancona in 1219,

Nave, north wall, first bay, Giotto (or Pietro Cavallini) and assistants, *Trial by Fire before the Sultan* (sc. XI)

during the Fifth Crusade, Francis finally landed in Egypt. Below the walls of Damietta which was under siege, where he also met John of Brienne, he had tried to get the Crusaders put an end to the war, which would be the cause of mourning and violence contrary to the Gospels. Ignored and probably put to flight after having predicted a defeat which then took place, Francis had to go into the Muslim field and had gone to Egypt, where he was warmly received, according to Bonaventure, by the sultan Malik el-Kamil (a generic name for it means "the king of camels"). He remained in Cairo for some time, where he attended the Koran schools and listened to lectures on Islamic philosophy. The *Legenda maior* narrates that in one of the long theological disputes in which he was involved, Francis was challenged to invoke the aid of his God to come unharmed out of the trial by fire. Tradition says that the Sultan prohibited the trial,

Nave, north wall, first bay, Giotto (or Pietro Cavallini) and assistants, *Ecstasy of Saint Francis* (sc. XII)

fearing that disorders and conversions might result if Francis won. In the scene shown however Bonaventure's story is modified and it is the Magi, the Islamic scholars, who shrink back and renounce the challenge. Probably the new version was more to the point, for the sultan, used to the sophisticated philological disquisitions of the School of Islam, would never have accepted a trial that was typical of the barbarian world (*ordalia*).

Scene XII) *The Ecstasy of Francis, and the acknowledgement of Christ's support of his mission*
Francis left Egypt because of the dissension that had broken out in Umbria among his followers and not because of difficulties encountered in his relationship with the Islamic intellectuals. The Franciscans were splitting into two factions – those who did not want to renounce a life of strict poverty (the Spirituals or Zealots) and those

Nave, north wall, Giotto (or Pietro Cavallini) and assistants, *Nativity Scene at Greccio* (sc. XIII)

who hoped for a monastic life for the Order (the Conventuals). Hastening back to Umbria, Francis, who had come into personal conflict with some of his followers, asked the new pope, Honorius III, to elect a General to head the Order and establish peace. The spiritual head of the Franciscans was still Francis but as difficulties with the Conventuals who wished to open schools and convents continued, Francis withdrew into solitude and abandoned his followers. With these bitter disagreements still fresh in the memory of those who commissioned the cycle in Assisi, the interpretation shown here tended to follow Bonaventure (X,l) who transformed that period of dissension and isolation for Francis into a moment of glorification. Alone in the forest, the Lord appeared to the Francis in ecstasy and the position of his arms, in the form of a cross, were a presentiment of the miracle of the stigmata. Recent analysis of the plaster in this scene have revealed that the cloud was added later so that the levitation of *Saint Francis* would not seem to be an 'error' in the rendering of space.

SCENE XIII
In the right-hand corner, near the entrance.
The Crib at Greccio or the *Reenactment of the Nativity scene with the Crib and the Coronation of the Christ Child*
The scene has recently been interpreted (Frugoni) as a message of hostility by Francis against the Crusades. In reenacting the birth of Christ in Greccio, Francis was saying that every place could be a new Bethlehem and that the birth of Jesus was a message of peace for all of mankind. Bonaventure (X,7) stressed the identification of Saint Francis with Christ, in line with orthodoxy, since the meaning of the birth and reincarnation of Christ could always be renewed. At Greccio Francis reenacted the scene of the Crib (Christ is always reborn in hearts after pardon). This custom would then become widespread and take on articulated form in the creation of the *Sacri Monti* set up to suggest Palestine. In this interpretation, the Franciscan message seemed to support the Crusades. The fact that the real Palestine, occupied by the Muslims, was missing made it necessary to create "surrogate" settings. Each Christmas therefore serves as a stimulus for the liberation of the Holy Places. As in the Franciscan tales, the scene takes place in Greccio by an altar set under a ciborium, with women peering in from behind a partition. It is the sanctuary of a church, subdivided as was usual at the time, by the iconostasis which separated the altar from the area reserved for the public and the women. The pulpit for the sermons was higher than the iconostasis. For many this is an extremely realistic representation, almost as if it were done from life, and may refer to a ceremony in the lower church of San Francesco, with Giunta Pisano's Cross shown above the iconostasis. It is difficult to decipher the heads of many of the figures because so much of the color has fallen.

b) Vertical reading of the wall: the *Old Testament* and *Saint Francis*
First register above divided by the window: on the left the *Sacrifice of Cain and Abel* [7] (destroyed) and, on the right the *Killing of Abel* [9] (fragmentary).
Middle register divided by the window: left *Joseph Thrown into the Well by his Brothers* [15] (or *Joseph Sold*, by the Pentecost Master or the young Giotto) and, on the right *Joseph Reveals Himself to his Brothers* [16] (or *Joseph's brothers in Egypt are pardoned by him*, by the Pentecost Master or the young Giotto).
A row of Saints are shown in the intrados of the arch. There are evident traces of repeated restoration and repainting, as in the neigh-

Nave, first bay, view of the north wall

boring *Stories of Joseph*, to which the "vinous shadows, the gray-green half tones, the large eyes circled in black and the dark bands around the cheeks" bear witness.

The message put forth in this bay deals with the struggle against the infidels who have abandoned the true Faith, and with betrayal. Both Muslims and Ghibellines were none other than Christians who had repudiated the true Faith to follow either Mohammed or the Emperor. The betrayal was detrimental to the Church, and Francis too had been betrayed by those who had abandoned him.

Scene XIII in the life of Saint Francis, seen in relation to the one above with Joseph pardoning his brothers, tends to underline the fact that after the betrayal there can always be a rebirth to new life through pardon for the entire world. As Joseph had pardoned his brothers, so with his birth which was renewed continuously, and with pardon, Christ had washed the sins of mankind of the Old Testament. With Francis this message was once more relevant.

c) Reading of the two walls (right and left) of the bay
Scheme of the representations:

NORTH WALL	SOUTH WALL
FIRST REGISTER	
Sacrifice of Cain and Abel [7]	*Dispute in the Temple* [7*]
Killing of Abel [8]	*Baptism of Christ* [8*]
MIDDLE REGISTER	
Joseph Thrown into the Well [15]	*Lamentation Over the Dead Christ* [15*]
Joseph Pardons his Brothers [16]	*The Three Marys at the Sepulcher* [16*]
FRANCISCAN REGISTER	
sc. X) *Expulsion of the Devils from Arezzo*	sc. XIX) *Receiving the Stigmata*

Left: Nave, first bay, view of the north wall
Right: Nave, first bay, view of the south wall

sc. XI) *Trial by Fire before the Sultan*

sc. XVIII) *Apparition at Arles*

sc. XII) *The Ecstasy of Saint Francis*

sc. XVII) *Sermon before Honorius III*

VAULT SECTIONS OVER THE FIRST BAY: the *Fathers of the Church*

In the vault on the west, towards the sanctuary, *Saint Gregory the Great* is shown. On the north is *Saint Ambrose.* The figure of *Saint Jerome*, which was in the east section of the vault near the main entrance, fell during the earthquake of 1997. On the south is *Saint Augustine.*

Nave, first bay, vault of the *Fathers of the Church* before the earthquake of 1997

Nave, first bay, detail of the vault of the *Fathers of the Church* with
Saint Jerome before the earthquake of 1997
Above: Nave, first bay, vault of the *Fathers of the Church* after the restoration done
after the earthquake of 1997

INNER FACADE

a) Horizontal reading of the scenes: the *Life of Saint Francis*

Nave, inner facade, detail

Neither Bonaventure's nor Thomas of Celano's order of events is respected in the scenes on the inner facade. Reference is to the miracles and preaching of the Saint, rather thorny questions. For Bonaventure, the *Miracle of the Spring* and, above all, the *Sermon to the Birds* had taken place near the end of Francis' life. For Thomas of Celano, it was the beginning. The problem in the first place then is chronological. These scenes undoubtedly act as a break in the succession of the stories and therefore seem to indicate that the inner facade was frescoed after the neighboring scenes on the right and left walls. This has also recently been confirmed by the analysis of the plaster by Bruno Zanardi, showing these panels to be completely independent of those next to them. But the problem is not only chronological, for over the decades numerous controversies have arisen regarding the question of the miracles of Francis.

Scene XIV) *The Miracle of the Spring* or

Nave, inner facade, Giotto (or Pietro Cavallini) and assistants, *The Miracle of the Spring* (sc. XIV)

Saint Francis bringing forth a new source of water
According to Bonaventure (VII,12) a long period of isolation had worn Francis out and on the way to La Verna with some of his companions he had caused water to gush forth in a mountainous site so that one of those accompanying him could slake his thirst. Aside from the miracle as such, which helped spread the fame of the saint and inspired Thomas of Celano to write a book about his *Miracles*, the universal message seemed rather clear: only faith was the certain source at which to drink, in line with various passages in the Gospels which Francis had clearly alluded to and which were then shown by the painter of this cycle. Giorgio Vasari, in the 16th century, was particularly impressed by the naturalism of this scene, and accurately described it in his *Lives* of 1568, highlighting the fact that it was "a thirsty man drinking who almost seemed a living person drinking" (*uno assetato che...bee...che par quasi una persona viva che bea*).

Scene XV) *Francis Preaching to the Birds*
The reconciliation of mankind and Creation through the preaching of Francis.
The scene of the *Sermon to the Birds* depicts one of the most difficult episodes in the life of Saint Francis, as does the preceding one. These events spring from the isolation into which Francis had withdrawn because his followers had deluded him. There were problems connected with the moment illustrated here, a moment known to all and handed down in an official version. Preaching, the celebration of Mass and the freeing from demons were reserved to the clergy and Francis had never embraced the ecclesiastical state. He had, however, preached at length but since these

Nave, inner facade, Giotto (or Pietro Cavallini) and assistants, *Sermon to the Birds* (sc. XV)

frescoes were celebrating his orthodoxy within the Church, this could not be referred to here. Francis is not shown preaching to the crowds in either the *Trial by Fire* or the *Crib in Greccio*, which depicted only the effects of his preaching (the confusion of the Magi and the devotion of those present). This is the only scene in which Francis sets forth his doctrine, basing himself on a passage in the Gospels where the Good Word was announced to all Creatures, and not by chance does he do this by turning to the birds, as in the

Nave, inner facade,
Ascension of Christ to Heaven

scene also frescoed in the lower church. Thomas of Celano considered this episode of great importance, for the birds could be identified with the poor and the weak. Bonaventure (XII,3) preferred to stress the analogy between the birds and all men, with a view to the universality of the Franciscan message. It is therefore not so much a miracle (except that the birds could really understand Francis), as it is a manifestation of love for Nature as in the *Canticle of Creatures*. Francis' hands are no longer in their original position, a change imposed by the conceptual problems involved, perhaps to de-emphasize the gestures.

Eagles are sculptured on the corner of the pedestals of the inner facade. As early as 1882 Fratini related them to a commission bestowed by Frederick II and recently (Cardini) it has been noted that eagles holding a hare are Guelph (and therefore also refer to Pope Gregory IX), while others believe them to refer to the emperor. Some of these eagles on the inner facade would then really be imperial emblems, together with the eagles and the crowned head in the transept which Nessi (1979) considered a portrait of Frederick.

b) Vertical reading of the wall: the *Church and Saint Francis*
First register above beneath the rose window: on the right is the *Ascension of Christ* [A] in the presence of Mary and the Apostles (the birth of the Church as the manifestation of the resurrected Christ in the world), forty days after the Resurrection. On the left is *Pentecost* [B], showing the descent of the Holy Spirit in the form of tongues of fire on the Apostles. Initially fearful and timid, they begin preaching and spreading the Gospel. This is the birth of the Church in its missionary activities.

Nave, view of the inner facade

Middle register above the entrance doors: on the left is *Saint Peter* [C], at the center the *Madonna and Child* [D] and, on the right *Saint Paul* [E].

This is the bay of Faith and the grace of God which performs miracles through the Church, of which *Mary, Saint Peter* and *Saint Paul* are the pilasters. On the left side water is celebrated as the element of salvation (*Saint Peter* fisherman of men after the miracle of the nets; *Saint Francis who brings forth a spring of water*); on the right preaching (*Saint Paul* the apostle of the people; *Saint Francis, the apostle of all creatures*). The mission of the primitive Church (*Christ, Mary, Saint John the Baptist* and the renewer *Saint Francis*) and of its organizers (the Fathers of the Church: *Saint Gregory the Great, Saint Ambrose, Saint Augustine, Saint Jerome*) are shown in the vaults of the nave, which was thought of in the Middle Ages as a '*Via Sacra*'. This liturgical itinerary is closed by the inner facade.

SOUTH (or LEFT WALL) OF THE NAVE: the identification of Francis with Christ and the problem of the stigmata

SCENE XVI
On the left-hand corner, near the entrance.
The Death of the Knight of Celano
This panel deals with the concept that it is to their advantage for lay persons to place the Franciscans under their protection, celebrating the sacrament of Confession.
According to Bonaventure's story (XI,4), Francis was invited to dinner by a Knight of Celano who wanted to enter the grace of the Lord through the words of the saint, after which the Knight died. This rather delicate iconographic passage actually attempts to furnish a theological explanation for an event which risked being slightly inconvenient. Francis is shown as a prophet who can predict death and therefore intercede before it takes place for the salvation of the soul, and with him his Order, which would have ensured prayer and comfort. The knight, shown stretched out and assisted by a woman, her fingers digging into her cheeks in sign of mourning, is seen dying, with *Francis and a follower* at table. The figure standing next to Francis was not originally meant to be a friar, but a lay figure or a prelate as indicated by the garments under the table where the folds do not correspond to that of a habit. The underlying reason is theological in nature, for since Francis was not ordained, he could not receive the confession of the knight before he died and an ordained monk had therefore to be included in the scene. Many art historians consider this episode a turning point in the Franciscan cycle of the upper church, for here and in the following scenes the style is more fully Gothic, in line with Angevin culture and the production of French illumination. Giovanni Pre-

Nave, south wall, Giotto (or Pietro Cavallini) and assistants, the *Death of the Knight of Celano* (sc. XVI)

vitali, one of the greatest scholars of this cycle, however tended to gloss over this difference, and explained it as an example of Giotto's skill in rendering a wide range of dramatical events.

FIRST BAY
a) Horizontal reading of the Franciscan register: the *Life of Saint Francis*

Nave, south wall, first bay, the frescoes of the register of the *Franciscan stories*

Scene XVII) *Francis Preaches Before Pope Honorius III* or the *Last Franciscan Rule*

The official birth of the Franciscan Order with the intercession of the Holy Spirit.

The final events in the story as told by Bonaventure (IV,11) are the approval of the last *Rule* by Pope Honorius III in 1223 and the official creation of the Order. This event is anticipated in the Assisi cycle, to show that subsequent events, in particular the highly controversial miracle of the stigmata, took place after, and not before, the Church had officially recognized the Order and Francis in person had obtained the papal stamp of approval. Actually the approval was the result of an extremely complicated compromise promoted by the future pope Gregory IX, in which the dissension within the Franciscan Order played a part. Moreover the more controversial aspects of the *Rule*, considered too subversive, had been toned down and the final document differed greatly from the original. Dissension within the Order continued, for the *Rule* now sanctioned the creation of the Order in its Conventual version, with the right to own property and receive income. From the Conventual point of view, this was then an episode of notable importance, and Bonaventure highlighted the fact that the Holy Spirit came in aid to *Francis* who found himself at a disadvantage before the scowling great *Prelates*. In its composition the scene is marked by the use of what by now was a scientific perspective in the construction of the architectural setting, a harbinger of the spatial 'conquests' of Humanism that were to follow. The painter was also careful to show the event in its 'historical' period, with realistic renderings of the costumes and features.

Scene XVIII) *The Apparition of Francis to the Brothers and to Anthony Preaching in the Chapter in Arles*

The creation of an autonomous Franciscan theological reflection.

The tale furnished by the Dominican Stefano di Bourbon of the discussion of the *Rule* by Francis before Pope Honorius III was quite different from the Franciscan version. The Dominican stressed the fact that Francis habitually preached to men and animals (which he could not do as a lay person or as the "simple and illiterate man" he was widely but mistakenly held to be). From an iconographic and narrative point of view, in the *Apparition of Francis in Arles* the Franciscan Chapter was offering a rebuttal to the accusations of their Dominican opponents, and their affirmations that Francis was a simple-minded person. In 1224 *Anthony*, one of Francis' followers, went to preach at the University in Arles, in France. This opened the world of culture to the Franciscans, on the

Nave, south wall, first bay, Giotto (or Pietro Cavallini) and assistants, *Saint Francis Preaching before Pope Honorius III* (sc. XVII)

basis of an interest that would become deeply felt in the following decades and which Francis had been very cautious about accepting in a university perspective (although he did later have contacts with the famous glossarist Irnerio di Bologna). His doubts were not so much a refusal of culture as such as a distrust of all the learned complications which might lead to a straying from the right way and cut off the understanding of the Word of God to the simpler people. In this scene the didactic and human aspects of the event are stressed, with the friars listening to Francis, almost as if each friar who announced his message could be a second Francis. Bonaventure (IV,10) on the other hand stressed the miraculous aspect of the event, describing Francis as floating in the air, just as the resurrected Christ had appeared to the Apostles.

Nave, south wall, first bay, Giotto (or Pietro Cavallini) and assistants, the *Apparition of Saint Francis to the Chapter in Arles* (sc. XVIII)

Scene XIX) *Francis Receiving the Stigmata on Monte La Verna*
The complete identification of Francis and Christ thanks to the signs of martyrdom (the stigmata).
The fulcrum of the identification of Francis with Christ takes place in this episode, narrated by his biographers in various versions, before that of Bonaventure (XIII,3). None of the saints who had identified with Christ before Francis had miraculously obtained the signs of physical suffering that marked Christ on the Cross (the signs of the nails, the crown of thorns and the wound on his side). It was Brother Elias who spread the news of the stigmata on the body of Francis immediately after his death. The ecclesiastical hierarchies however were always rather perturbed, despite the fact that a few years after Francis' death Pope Gregory

Nave, south wall, first bay, Giotto (or Pietro Cavallini) and assistants, *Saint Francis Receiving the Stigmata* (sc. XIX)

IX had declared them to be authentic. The Franciscans themselves were suspicious of the stigmata. In his two *Lives of Francis* Thomas of Celano changed versions as to the nature of the prodigy, claiming at the end that at La Verna Francis had seen a seraph with the stigmata, but that he himself did not have them. Pope Alexander IV (nephew of Gregory IX), who had been one the patron Cardinals of the Order and had been present at the death of Francis, said he had verified the stigmata and in a letter of 1255 officially accepted the parallel between Francis and Christ, so the Franciscans could not be accused of heresy. The presence of the stigmata on the body of Francis had already been maintained in the *Vita secunda* by Thomas of Celano in 1246, conferred on him by an angel-seraph on the mountain of La Verna. The tradition was then also adopted in the *Legenda maior* by Bonaventure da Bagnoregio in 1263 (and in 1266 replaced the story in the *Vita secunda*). For Saint Bonaventure the stigmata on the body of Francis were the sign of his complete identification with Christ, who had personally given them. In this scene, the controversial question as to how he actually received the stigmata is resolved by placing the crucified Christ within the angelic wings of the Seraph. Rays from the figure of Christ transmit their tangible sign to Francis. In the Bardi Chapel in Santa Croce in Florence, Giotto showed Christ directly conferring the wounds on Francis. The question of the stigmata however continued to be the object of debate, despite papal approval, and not long after, the founder of the Dominican Order, Saint Dominic, also had the stigmata (as did Saint Catherine of Siena and, most recently, Padre Pio, the 'new Saint Francis' of the 20th century). Serious doubts have recently been advanced (Frugoni) regarding the reality of the stigmata of Saint Francis, highlighting the fact that the tradition was important for the legitimization of the Order. Here Francis appears as an "antique hero", almost as if he were an immobile statue in the midst of a harsh wild Nature.

b) Vertical reading of the wall: Saint Francis and the episodes of the *Life of Christ*

First register above divided by the window: on the right the *Dispute in the Temple* [7*] (fragmentary); on the left, the *Baptism of Jesus in the Jordan* [8*] (fragmentary).

Middle register divided by the window: on the right: *Lamentation over the Dead Christ* [15*] (attributed to Giotto); left, the *Three Marys at the Sepulcher* [16*] (fragmentary).

The scene of the *Lamentation* seems to represent an intermediate moment between the *Deposition* and the *Burial of Christ*, in which the body of the dead Christ is being adored. The difference of the levels on which the figures are set was suggested both by a hierarchic view of the figures themselves and by the chronology of the happenings. The *three Marys* in the background arrived after those who had been closest to the living Christ had rendered him homage. The two richly dressed figures, whose features are not recognizable, may be the centurion *Longinus* (who in the Gospels was converted in the presence of the dead Christ after he had wounded him in the ribs, which then became one of the stigmata) or *Nicodemus*. In the foreground are the *three Marys*, with the halo of sanctity, the *Virgin Mary* and *Saint John*. The anti-perspective placing of the body of Christ serves to make his wounds clearly visible, to cor-

Nave, first bay, view of the south wall

respond to the stigmata in the death of Saint Francis in the lower Franciscan register.

This is the bay of the receiving of the Grace of God and of Wisdom: Francis in receiving the stigmata enters the ranks of the Saints. But the identification of Francis with Christ also deals with Wisdom: Christ disputing in the Temple with the Priests, teaches His Truth, and Francis has to have his Rule approved by Pope Honorius, disputing with the Cardinals. If the poorly preserved figure in the *Lamentation over the Dead Christ* [15*] is really *Longinus* then *Francis Receiving the Stigmata* below would be closely connected to the scene above.

SECOND BAY

a) Horizontal reading of the Franciscan register: the *Death of Francis*

Nave, south wall, second bay, the frescoes of the register of the *Franciscan stories*

These three panels bears witness to the outbreak of a new figurative trend which crowds the scenes with figures. Various painters worked on these frescoes and stylistically speaking the figures are more elegant and the buildings more fully Gothic.

Scene XX) *The Death of Saint Francis, and the vision of his ascension to heaven*
After receiving the stigmata, Francis was marked by martyrdom and according to Bonaventure (XIV,6) could now die. The scene is played out in two levels: below, the terrestrial world shows the *Saint's body* laid out on a rough board and surrounded by eleven of his distraught followers (like the eleven Apostles after Judas committed suicide), clerics and others. The scene is that of the exhibition of the body after his death. The problematical question of the benediction he imparted is glossed over. Just to whom he gave it is not known. Was it Brother Elias, of the Conventual branch of the Order, the man who initiated the great undertaking of the construction of the Basilica? Or was it Bernardo, closer to the original meaning of Franciscanism and therefore head of the Spirituals? The problem was similar to that of *Isaac's blessing*, extorted by Jacob.

Nave, south wall, second bay, Giotto (or Pietro Cavallini) and assistants, the *Death of Saint Francis* (sc. XX)

Above, in the second level, *Francis in Glory* has risen to Heaven supported by *angels* above a cloud, and with the visible signs of the stigmata on his hands and rib (the tunic is torn at one side). A brother is said to have had this vision and the ascent of Francis to Heaven was like that of a brilliant star.

Scene XXI) *The Apparition of Saint Francis to Brother Agostino and the Bishop of Assisi*

In this scene two episodes which took place at the same time when Francis died, according to the story told by Saint Bonaventure (XIV,6), but in different places, are synthesized. On the left, *Agostino*, who had been nominated Minister of the Franciscans in Campania, and his brothers are shown in the great church with its three aisles. The friar, who was ill and could no longer speak, suddenly woke up just as Francis was dying (he is shown seated on a bed) and

Nave, south wall, second bay, Giotto (or Pietro Cavallini) and assistants, the *Vision of the Death of Saint Francis* (sc. XXI)

exclaimed: "wait for me Father, I am coming with you" before he himself died. A 'remote control' prodigy therefore. At the same time the *Bishop of Assisi*, on the right, who at the time was in Frederick's territories in Puglia, in the sanctuary of Saint Michael in Monte Sant'Angelo (where Francis had also gone), had the vision of the death of Francis in a dream and then verified the contemporaneity of the death with his dream: a second prodigy which served to diffuse 'by remote control' the fame of Francis about to become a saint. Integration in pencil of the features of the brother on the extreme left of the scene (where the intonaco had fallen) may be due to restoration dating to 1938-1940.

Scene XXII) *Confirmation of the Stigmata on the Body of Francis by a Lay Person*
The scene once more refers to the controversial reality of the stig-

Nave, south wall, second bay, Giotto (or Pietro Cavallini) and assistants, *Confirmation of the Stigmata* (sc. XXII)

mata on the body of Francis. The episode, which was particularly useful in the debates against those who belittled the figure of the Saint, had been told only by Bonaventure (XV,4). All the citizens had come to the chapel of the Porziuncola (in the basilica of Santa Maria degli Angeli), including the Franciscan friars and the *Knight Jerome*, who as he knelt had put his fingers in the wound on Francis' ribs to make sure it was real. The analogy with the gospel story is evident and the incredulous *Knight*, according to Bonaventure, is seen as a new Saint Thomas who had doubted the resurrection of Christ. According to the tale though the event had taken place outside, near the Porziuncola, where the body was exhibited. To be noted is the setting which refers to the interior of a building in which the large decorated beam has icons of the *Archangel Michael* and of the *Madonna Enthroned* on top, as well as a great *Crucifix* at the center. It does not seem to be the same Crucifix of San Damiano in scene I (*Christus triumphans*), but rather the new *Christus patiens*, that is the suffering Christ, as already shown by Giunta Pisano in the *Cross* that has been lost. This setting may therefore allude to the construction of the lower church, or a real Franciscan sanctuary (perhaps initially at Santa Maria degli Angeli).

Nave, second bay, view of the south wall

b) Vertical reading of the wall: the *Death of Saint Francis* and the *Death of Christ*

The first register above divided by the window: on the right the *Presentation in the Temple for the Circumcision* [5*] (by the Maestro della Cattura); on the left, the *Flight into Egypt* [6*] (fragmentary).

Middle register divided by the window: on the right, *Way to Calvary* [13*] (Maestro della Cattura); on the left, *Crucifixion* [14*] (perhaps by a Tuscan painter).

This bay celebrates the death of Christ and that of Francis, after having repeatedly stressed the complete identification of the two. Bonaventure's tale emphasized the fact that the living Francis conformed to the living Christ, and after his death conformed to the dying Christ. If then the *Death of Francis* corresponds to the *Crucifixion and Death of Christ*, then the *Presentation at the Temple of Jesus,* when he is circumcised as a symbol of his belonging to the Elect, corresponds to the *Confirmation of the Stigmata of Francis*, the tangible element of his sainthood and his supernatural nature; while Salvation, achieved by the strenuous *Flight to Egypt*, has its companion piece in the *Ascension of Francis* after his death, the crowning of eternal Salvation.

THIRD BAY
a) Horizontal reading of the Franciscan register:
mourning the death of Francis and his canonization

Nave, south wall, third bay, the frescoes of the register with the *Franciscan stories*

Scene XXIII) *The Mourning of the Poor Clares, and the leave-taking of Clare from the body of Francis*

In this scene the body of Francis is shown for the last time. It is here embraced by *Saint Clare*, already canonized at the time the cycle was being painted as shown by the halo around her head.

The presence of Clare is fundamental, once more, in proving the

Nave, south wall, third bay, Giotto (or Pietro Cavallini) and assistants, *Mourning of the Poor Clares* (sc. XXIII)

reality of the stigmata, for the Saint was taken as an authoritative source. For Bonaventure (XV,5), Clare was a sort of mute witness to the stigmata, while for Thomas of Celano it was Jacopa dei Settesoli who affirmed the truth of the miracle after Brother Elias had fallen into disgrace. But Jacopa was a lay person, so that in the fresco it was preferable to replace her with *Clare*, reaffirming also her close bonds with Francis. The saint is shown in a pose which was typical of the Virgin Mary or the pious Women in sacred iconography. The building on the right from which the Clares are coming is of particular interest. Could it have been an idea for the building of the Franciscan sanctuary church at the Porziuncola, as also seems to be indicated by the scene of the *Death of Saint Francis?* The spotting of the colors of the drapery on which Francis lies, as well as the lower part of the catafalque, bear witness to the vicissitudes the basilica was subject to over the centuries. These are probably the signs, in particular the red spots, of a terrible fire that broke out in the nave.

Scene XXIV) *The Canonization of Saint Francis*
The miracles of the saint or encouragement to go and make the pilgrimage to Assisi.
The feast of the canonization of Saint Francis was celebrated in July 1228 by Pope Gregory IX. This scene depicts the official ceremony which took place in Piazza del Comune in Assisi. The pope was probably on the baldachin/balcony on the left, above, but this zone is now completely illegible. Below are *mothers* with sick *children*, like the girl set under the table, who are waiting for some miracle connected with the sanctification of Francis. Various tales of his life do tell us of the healing the Saint accomplished, but once more the iconographical abbreviation changed the historical succession of events. The miracle of the healing of the girl took place when Francis was buried, and thereafter became a story passed by word of mouth. To make the canonization of Francis even more outstanding, this famous episode which served as example to pilgrims and stressed his fame as a healer, was added to a scene which took place two years later. Bonaventure (XV,7) glossed over this miracle, which took place in the church of San Giorgio where Francis was buried before 1230. The new Franciscan Basilica had no similar miracle which could certify the fact that Francis "approved" of the building (this aspect was fundamental in the debate between the Spirituals, who opposed the construction of a new shrine, and the Conventuals). As a result neither the caption nor the depiction clearly show where the miracle took place, and neither the church of San Giorgio nor the Piazza del Comune are shown (in opposition to the clarity of setting in the scene of the *Renouncement of Worldly Goods*). The considerable areas where color has fallen, and the red spots in the lower zone, show that this scene too must have been damaged, like the preceding, in a fire.

Scene XXV) *The Apparition of Francis to Pope Gregory IX, who was initially incredulous of the reality of the stigmata and is now convinced by the Saint*
This prodigious apparition of Francis to Pope Gregory IX appears only in the appendix to the *Legenda maior* by Bonaventure (in the chapter *De miraculis* based on Thomas of Celano). This was before Francis' canonization, since the Pope had serious doubts as to the reality of the stigmata. Despite the severe tone of the *Saint* and the evidence of the wounds on his hands, Gregory was not completely

Nave, south wall, third bay, Giotto (or Pietro Cavallini) and assistants, the *Canonization of Saint Francis* (sc. XXIV)

convinced and during the ceremony made no mention of the fact. Then he turned the question over to his nephew, later also to become pope as Alexander IV, but he waited until 1237 to officially express his recognition of the reality of this prodigy. At the end of the 13th century when the iconographic program as a whole was perfected, this panel was turned over to the *Dream of Gregory IX* to symbolize the evidence of the stigmata, but also the resistance opposed by many sectors of the Church. *Gregory* touched the wounds, but continued sleeping. It is no coincidence that this scene is below the one of *Christ before Pilate*, where the ancient Roman Governor refused to take a clear position regarding Christ. In addition to the depiction of the drapery hanging on the wall in the papal alcove (in continuity with the analogous scenes beginning

Nave, south wall, third bay, Giotto (or Pietro Cavallini) and assistants, *Saint Francis Appearing to Pope Gregory IX* (sc. XXV)

with the *Stories of Isaac*), of particular interest is the rendering of the coffering in the ceiling, which anticipated the use of one point perspective in the 15th century.

b) Vertical reading of the wall: Saint Francis and the episodes of the *Life of Christ*
First register above divided by the window: on the right the *Nativity* [3*] (or the *Manger Scene* by the Maestro della Cattura); on the left, the *Adoration of the Magi* [4*] (or *Epiphany*, fragmentary).
Middle register divided by the window: on the right, the *Capture of Christ* [11*] (or the *Betrayal by Judas* by the Maestro della Cattura): on the left, *Christ before Pilate* [12*] (or the *Flagellation*, fragmentary.
The two principal themes of this series are those of the Birth and

Nave, third bay, view of the south wall

the Adoration: as *Christ was born on Earth* so with the *Canonization* Francis is born to new life, that of the Saints, after his death. The *Mourning of the Poor Clares,* then, is simply analogous to the *Adoration of Jesus by the Magi.*

Left: Nave, south wall, third bay, upper register, Maestro della Cattura, *Nativity;* *right:* Nave, south wall, third bay, middle register, Maestro della Cattura, *Taking of Christ*

FOURTH BAY
a) Horizontal reading of the Franciscan register: the miracles of the Franciscan faith

Nave, south wall, fourth bay, the frescoes of the register of the *Franciscan stories*

Scene XXVI) *The Immediate Healing of a Devoted Follower (John of Lerida in Catalonia), an example of the miracles of Saint Francis in foreign lands*
Francis, accompanied by two *Angels,* saves a *mortally wounded believer* from death in Catalonia. His miracles of healing also take place in far distant cities. Just as the dying man's wife, discouraged, is about to leave the room, he is freed from suffering thanks to the strength of his devotion and the thaumaturgic power of the stigmata, which *Francis* imposes on him. The Dominicans and the clergy in Spain were particularly reluctant to accept the reality of

Nave, south wall, fourth bay, Giotto (or Pietro Cavallini) and assistants, the *Healing of John of Lerida* (sc. XXVI)

the stigmata and publicly declared the followers of Francis to be "heretics". Once again note the precise perspective rendering of the room, not only in the walls but above all in the coffering of the ceiling.

Scene XXVII) *The Confession of a Woman Brought Back to Life: a Franciscan friar confesses a woman on Monte Merano in Benevento who was brought back to life after having died*

In this scene the miracle of resurrection is not accomplished directly by Saint Francis, but through his intercession, upon request of a Franciscan friar. Francis is shown above on the left adoring the Lord (note the Saint's foot with the stigmata showing below his tunic). The family of the deceased woman who has just come back to life and is confessing to the *friar*, observe the scene and alternate gestures of devotion with expressions of amazement and joy. The raising of the dead, as was the case with Jesus and Lazarus, represents one of the most marvelous miracles and Bonaventure devotes great

Nave, south wall, fourth bay, Giotto (or Pietro Cavallini) and assistants, the *Confession of the Woman Brought Back to Life* (sc. XXVII)

attention to these episodes in his *De miraculis*. But the scene also stresses the fully ecclesiastical role of the Franciscans, for it is one of them who administers the sacrament of Confession. It is no coincidence that this prodigious event took place in Campania (see also scene XXI of the *Vision of Brother Agostino*) where the Order had a strong following. Since the Angevin dynasty in Naples was very close to the Franciscans, the Campanian setting of the miracle was particularly important in this period. Unfortunately much color has fallen from this panel and large portions are badly abraded. This side of the basilica had been particularly subject to damage over the centuries.

Scene XXVIII) *The Liberation of the Penitent Heretic: Saint Francis frees Pietro di Alife who had been accused of heresy and unjustly imprisoned*
A citizen of Alife, near Caserta in Campania, was accused of heresy and put in prison. *Saint Francis*, flying in on the left, frees him from

Nave, south wall, fourth bay, Giotto (or Pietro Cavallini) and assistants, *Saint Francis Freeing Peter of Alife* (sc. XXVIII)

his chains in the presence of a throng of notables and the Bishop who is kneeling and praying to the Saint. The scene recalls the liberation of Saint Peter, imprisoned, just like this Peter, for having preached the resurrected Christ. Angels broke the chains and opened the gates of his prison. This explains the fact that the prison shown on the left is a circular building with a tower decorated with a relief frieze of scenes of war, a clear allusion to the spiral columns of Trajan and Marcus Aurelius in Rome. The many-storied building on the right recalls the Septizonium, another famous antiquity of Rome. These allusions to the Roman and Campanian ambience clearly refer to the Angevin policies, at the time profoundly pro-papal. Yet the court of Naples also supported Saint Thomas, and the Dominicans, the most outspoken accusers of the Franciscan "heresy". It was at this time that the fundamental theological considerations of Saint Thomas saw the light. In 1277 the Franciscans and the house of Anjou had succeeded in expelling Thomas from Naples, although he was later was readmitted.

Nave, fourth bay, view of the south wall

b) Vertical reading of the wall: the miracles of Saint Francis and those in the *Life of Christ*

The first register above divided by the window: on the right the *Annunciation* [1*] (perhaps by Jacopo Torriti); on the left the *Visitation* [2*] (destroyed).

Middle register divided by the window: on the right, the *Wedding in Cana* [9*] (perhaps by Jacopo Torriti, but the obvious repainting

Nave, south wall, fourth bay, middle register, Jacopo Torriti, *Wedding of Cana*

makes any real hypotheses as to the artist impossible); on the left, the *Raising of Lazarus* [10*] (perhaps by Jacopo Torriti, fragmentary).

This is the wall of Miracles and Resurrections: we find the *Miracle of the Annunciation* with, above all, that of the *Visitation*, of the *Raising of Lazarus*, the *Wedding in Cana*, to which Francis' miracles of the *Bringing Back to Life of a Woman of Monte Merano* and the *Liberation of Pietro di Alife* correspond.

THE FLOOR OF THE UPPER CHURCH

Up to the early 1940s the floor of the upper church was brick, which enhanced the richness of the frescoes on the walls and vaulting. As a result of a *Convention on Architectural History* held in Assisi, a commission was set up by the Fascist minister of the time, Giuseppe Bottai, to study the state of preservation of the frescoes.

Detail of the floor in white and pink Assisi marble

These scientific analyses then led to the creation of the Istituto Centrale del Restauro in Rome. Gustavo Giovannoni, the leading scholar on restoration at the time, summed up the situation. The new studies showed that the damage was mostly due to the humidity which seeped into the Basilica (for which Cavalcaselle had already tried to find a remedy). On the walls this humidity created a "patina which merged and mitigated the colors and might seem to be an element which enhanced the appreciation of the work of art but which was, instead, not a safeguard, but an enemy which had to be dealt with". The restorer Pelliccioli was entrusted with accurately washing all the surfaces with the Cavenaghi method, that is by "applying moist towels on the walls which, after having been pressed, were taken off without rubbing them on the surface; the work was patiently continued until the patina was eliminated...But not one of the retouchings in *fresco secco* was altered [so unlike what was removed from the Lorenzetti frescoes in the lower church, twenty years later], not one of the figures was even slightly repainted... The restoration was simply a washing, which revived the colors of the frescoes". A second, highly important, intervention concerned the floor of the building, since it was decided to "build the floor of the church in marble, instead of brick, to exclude the principal cause of dust which would be deposited on the walls and would once more have covered them with incrustations. The floor was laid in white and pink Assisi marble, in various patterns taken from those in the lower church...The serene color and the minute pattern kept this new element in a minor key and did not compete with the frescoes on the walls which had to remain, and which did remain, the protagonists".

A Fascist *fasces* or symbol and the date near the high altar mark the end of the work, bearing witness to a period of architectural restoration which played an important role in defining the present aspect of the Basilica.

Upper Church, *Saint Francis and Saint Anthony*, details of the two-light window to the right of the entrance to the nave

SELECTED GENERAL BIBLIOGRAPHY

– CAVALCASELLE, G.B. and CROWE J.A., *A New History of Italian Painting*, London, 1864 (*Storia della pittura in Italia*, it. ed. Florence, 1876).
– OFFNER, R., "Giotto-non Giotto", *The Burlington Magazine*, I, LXXIV, 1939, 259-268.
– PELLICCIOLI, A., "I restauri della Basilica Superiore di Assisi. Relazione alla Commissione ministeriale", *Le Arti*, V, 1941-1942, 216-221.
– GIOVANNONI, G., "Assisi. Chiesa Superiore di San Francesco [i restauri]", *Palladio*, I, 1941, 36-38.
– PREVITALI, G., *Giotto e la sua Bottega*, Milan, 1974 (2d. revised ed.).
– LUNGHI, E., "Tematiche e committenze pittoriche in età barocca", in *Arte e musica in Umbria tra Cinquecento e Seicento*, Spoleto, 1981.
– ROCCHI, G., *La basilica di San Francesco ad Assisi*, Florence, 1982.
– *Pittura in Umbria tra il 1480 e il 1540. Premesse e sviluppi nei tempi di Perugino e Raffaello*, Catalog of the exhibition, Perugia, 1983.
– BELLOSI, L., *La pecora di Giotto*, Turin, 1985
– BONELLI, R., "Specialis Ecclesia": ipotesi sulle fasi costruttive della basilica di Assisi, *Architettura, Storia e Documenti*, 2, 1985, 5-33.
– TODINI, F., "Pittura del Duecento e del Trecento in Umbria e il cantiere di Assisi" in *La pittura in Italia. Il Duecento e il Trecento*, Milan, 1986, 375-413.
– ZERI, F., *La collezione Federico Mason Perkins*, Turin, 1988.
– BERG, D., "L'impero degli Svevi e il gioachimismo francescano" in *L'attesa della fine dei tempi nel Medioevo*, Bologna, 1990, 133-167.
– DELLA PORTA, P.M., GENOVESI E., LUNGHI E., *Guida di Assisi. Storia e arte*, Assisi, 1992[2]
– LUNGHI, E., "Tematiche e committenze pittoriche in età barocca", in *Assisi in età barocca*, ed. by A. GROHMANN, Assisi, Accademia Properziana del Subasio, 1992, 367-388.
– BARONE, G., "La propaganda anti-imperiale nell'Italia federiciana: l'azione degli Ordini mendicanti", in *Federico II e le città italiane*, ed. by P. TOUBERT and A. PARAVICINI BAGLIANI, Palermo, 1994, 278-289.
– NESSI, S., *La Basilica di San Francesco e la sua documentazione storica*, Assisi, 1994.
– SCHENKLUHN, W., *San Francesco in Assisi: ecclesia specialis*, Milan, 1994.
– LUNGHI, E., "Presenza di Federico II nella chiesa di San Francesco ad Assisi", in *Assisi al tempo di Federico II, in Atti dell'Accademia Properziana del Subasio*, 23, 1995, 213-243.
– FRUGONI, C. and ZANARDI B., *Il cantiere di Giotto. Le Storie di San Francesco ad Assisi*, Milan, 1996.
– VOLPE, C., *Pietro Lorenzetti*, ed. by M. LUCCO, Milan, 1996.
– BELLOSI, L., *Cimabue*, ed. by P. RAGIONIERI, Milan, 1998.

Upper Church, Christ the *Redeemer with Francis* and the *Virgin Mary with the Child*,
detail of the two-light window to the left of the entrance to the nave

CONTENTS

LIFE OF SAINT FRANCIS 4

COMPLEX OF THE PILGRIMAGE CHURCH OF SAINT FRANCIS
- History of the building of the Franciscan complex 24
- Former Oratory of San Bernardino 43
- Entrance porch to the Lower Church 54

LOWER CHURCH 54
- Altar 82
- Apse 82
- Campanile 93
- Cantoria 58
- Chiostro dei Morti or Cemetery 60
- Choir stalls 83
- Monument to John of Brienne 59
- Narthex (known also as Atrium or Gallery) 55
- Nave 65
- Sacristy, lower 93
- Sacristy, hidden 93
- Tomb of Giovanni Gaetano Orsini 105
- Tomb of the Cerchi 57
- Transept, north 94
- Transept, south 84
- Tribune or pulpit of Saint Stanislas 73
CHAPELS IN THE LOWER CHURCH
- Sant'Antonio Abate 60
- Sant'Antonio da Padova 110
- Santa Caterina 60
- Fontana Chapel 122
- San Giovanni Battista 85
- San Lorenzo 113
- Santa Maria Maddalena 106
- San Martino 113
- San Nicola 102
- San Pietro d'Alcantara (or Sant'Andrea) 122
- San Sebastiano 57
- Santo Stefano 113
- San Valentino 110
CRYPT (TOMB OF SAINT FRANCIS) 122

SACRO CONVENTO
- CHAPTER ROOM or Chapel of the Relics 124

– Chiostro Grande or of Sixtus IV 12

– Library of the Convent .... 1?

– Loggiato del "Calzo" 4

– Museo del Tesoro 12

– Perkins Collection... 1?

Upper Church .... 13?

– Floor of the Basilica .... 2?

– Inner facade 2c

– Nave 16

Transept .... 13?

– Altar .... 15?

– Apse 14

– Choir stalls .... 15?

– Papal throne .... 1?

– Transept, north arm 15

– Transept, south arm 14

Bibliography .... 23?

We should particularly like to thank Father Gerhard Ruf
of the Sacro Convento of Assisi
for his collaboration and invaluable advice

The suggestions and corrections furnished by Maria Brigliadori Canali,
Virgilio Galati, Gastone Petrini
and Giorgio Zuliani have also been of invaluable help

© Copyright by Bonechi Edizioni 'Il Turismo' S.r.l.
Via dei Rustici, 5 - 50122 FLORENCE
Tel. +39-055 239.82.24
Fax +39-055 21.63.66
E-mail: barbara@bonechi.com
           bbonechi@dada.it
http://www.bonechi.com
All rights reserved
Printed in Italy

Editorial chief: Barbara Bonechi
Editorial coordination, revision and iconographical research: Lorena Lazzari
Translation: Studio Comunicare
Layout: Nunzia Trabucco and Sabrina Menicacci
Cover and plans graphic art: Nunzia Trabucco
Drawings: Virgilio Galati
All plans were originally designed by: Ferruccio Canali and Virgilio Galati
Photo credits: – Archives Bonechi Edizioni 'Il Turismo' S.r.l., by
                 Nicola Grifoni, Florence - Giorgio Deganello, Padua
                 Marco Rabatti, Florence - Giuseppe Carfagna, Rome
              – Photographic Archives Sacro Convento di Assisi taken by
                 Father Gerhard Ruf
Aerial photographs: Cornelio Timpani Image Edition, Florence:
                 CONCESSION S.M.A. No. 307 of 30/6/94
                 CONCESSION S.M.A. No. 195 of 15/6/95
Photolithography: Fotolito Immagine, Florence
Printing: BO.BA.DO.MA, Florence
ISBN 88-7204-447-2